Sacred Space at Home

Architecture with Soul

Anne Knorr

Sacred Space at Home

Architecture with Soul
by Anne Knorr

HomeDesign Publishing
Boulder, CO 80305

Printed in the United States of
America

Library of Congress Control Number:
2012917219

ISBN-978-0-615-69892-2

Contents

Introduction:

Architecture and Spirit

The journey that led me to explore the connection between architecture and spirituality began several years ago when I participated in a 13-month program for spiritual directors in Denver, Colorado. During the program, a group of 15 participants met at a local convent several weekends throughout the year to learn the subtle art of accompanying a person on his or her spiritual path. Over the course of our time together we were asked to offer our expertise in an hour-long presentation to the group, presumably relating to spiritual direction. Since the majority of my professional training had been in residential architecture, I wasn't sure how to relate my background designing homes with spiritual direction. Though I was keenly aware of the profound impact our living spaces have on our sense of physical well-being, until that moment I hadn't considered the many ways our environment, particularly our home, mirrors and supports our spiritual well-being.

Intrigued by the notion that a relationship exists between architecture and spirituality, I began to explore the idea of sacred space. As a child I remember sneaking into the musty attic of my Midwestern home with my brother and sister to rummage through trunks of old clothes, photographs of distant relatives, and family heirlooms tucked into boxes. A sword dating back to the civil war era that belonged to my great-grandfather especially captivated us, and we would gingerly pull it from its sheath exposing a shiny metal edge. It was as if we had entered a secret world all our own, a sacred childhood space. My natural curiosity, imagination, and spirit were seamlessly intertwined with my surroundings—I intuitively knew how to find or create a space that nurtured my soul. This is a common childhood experience, whether it's building a fort from cardboard boxes, hiding out in the leafy branches of a tree, or burrowing under the security of a quilt. We all have an innate ability to find sacred space. There is a common shared experience or archetypal quality to this pattern of seeking and finding sacred places. Indigenous people often found it in nature and eventually altars and sanctuaries were built to mark these special places. I wondered if early sanctuaries might reveal something more about the relationship between our spirit and the physical forms we create.

Drawn to an ancient tent structure called the Tabernacle, a place early nomadic Jewish people worshipped God, I found what I was looking for. Why this structure popped into my head I don't know, but I like to think it was Divine guidance. Over forty chapters in their sacred books described in detail how to build the Tabernacle. I was curious why so much text was devoted to building a tent, so I decided to look at the Tabernacle through the eyes of an architect, paying close attention to the different areas that made up the structure and the flow of circulation through it. A pattern in the layout of the Tabernacle became clear. It was comprised of three main spaces: a public courtyard where the tribes of Israel gathered, a private place within the tent for the priests, and an intimate place where only the high priest entered. Each space had unique qualities, yet there was a fluid movement weaving through them that bound them together. I started to see how this simple pattern of three could be applied to the places where we live. I was particularly struck by the need for individual space within a home.

The pattern goes beyond the physical realm and speaks to the interior space of spirit as well. Like the Tabernacle, our interior sanctuary needs to include spaces that are public, private, and intimate. Our lives are enriched when we interact with others in community but also when we allow time for stillness and time to be with those we love. As we move across the continuum between activity and solitude, we can find a balance that resonates with our soul. When the spaces in our home mirror our personal inclinations, we feel supported both physically and spiritually. Being in community may energize some of us, while time alone may nourish others. Regardless of our leaning, to feel at peace in our dwelling and within our self, all three spaces need to be present. The particular configuration of these spaces is unique for each of us, but the more our home follows the pattern of the Tabernacle and is attuned to our personal rhythms, the more it will feel like sacred space.

The first chapters of this book explore our intuitive understanding of sacred space in more detail and the archetypal patterns that help articulate what it is. Along with the pattern of three, doorways, rituals, meaningful objects, prayer, and beauty are important elements to consider. Architectural basics about scale, proportion, color, and light are discussed in later chapters as well as principles of Feng Shui.

The final chapter offers practical suggestions for transforming your home into a personal sanctuary by incorporating focal points, mindful placement of furniture, and above all, engaging a sense of play. This book can be used as a workbook if you choose to engage the exercises at the end of each chapter, or you can simply read to broaden your understanding of sacred space. There is space at the end of each chapter for taking a few notes but a journal or sketch pad will be needed for the exercises. Many of the photographs and examples are taken from my experience as an architect designing custom homes. I want this material to be accessible to

people from all walks of life, regardless
of financial resources. When applicable,
I have included alternative solutions that
are more modest in scale. My hope is the
guiding principles found in the Tabernacle
will enrich your dwelling, particularly the
notion of making space for yourself.

Anne Knorr

My house feeds my spirit...

~Sarah Susanka

Chapter 1

Rediscovering an Intuitive Sense of Sacred Space

The magical child is the part of us that is pure and innocent; the child that was untouched by the external experience of growing up.

~ Wayne Kritsberg
Author & psychologist

Early Experiences of Sacred Space

What makes a place sacred, set apart from the ordinary? When we were children, sacred space emerged organically from our play while building forts from pillows and blankets, discovering a secret corner in the attic to read, or climbing a maple tree to hide among the branches overlooking the world below. Following our creative impulses, we transformed ordinary furniture, tossed-out boxes, or overgrown hedges into magical new worlds that nurtured our sense of well-being, as if our inner compass recognized our need for a sacred place and we intuitively found a way to create it. When we were children, our creative process included an openness of heart that lacked the judgment or criticism we often adopt as adults. The text of the Bible sums it up this way, "To enter the kingdom of heaven you must become like a child," (Matthew 18:3) alluding to the simple yet often profound understanding children possess about spiritual matters.

When creating a sacred space for our self, rekindling the wisdom from childhood is a powerful tool. The following story describes one woman's experience as she remembers her childhood sacred space.

I met Christie a few months before she was released from the Denver Women's Correctional Facility where she was incarcerated for several years. She later moved into a halfway house and now lives in an apartment overlooking a park with large cottonwood trees, meandering paths, and picnic tables scattered across an open field of grass. The front of her apartment building faces a busy boulevard where she catches a bus each day to the grocery store where she works. Twice a month we meet at a local cafe for a light breakfast, hot coffee, and conversation. My role in her life is to be a listener and spiritual mentor. Tucked away in a corner booth we discuss the details of her daily life that challenge her as she faces re-entering society or creating a budget. Her face glows when she tells me about passing her high school equivalency test or being promoted at work. Christie also shares about God's presence in her life and the gratitude she feels for beginning a new chapter in her life free of addiction.

The country-style restaurant is a welcome change from the sparse office where we met at the prison. Soft fabric seats, a table with flowers, and the background hum of conversation and clanking dishes replace plastic chairs, a Formica desk, linoleum floors, and a locked door. At one of our sessions, Christie appeared anxious. In a week, she would be leaving the halfway house and moving into her own apartment, and the prospect of living independently was frightening. She was excited about regaining some freedom in her life but intimidated by the added responsibilities she would face. Though she longed for the privacy and solitude the apartment would provide, the thought of losing the familiarity of a structured environment with strict schedules, rules, and supervision felt overwhelming. As I listened to Christie, I could hear her fear and anxiety mounting. I offered her a simple meditation to reframe the situation as she remembered her first experience of a sacred place.

Memories of her grandmother's couch, the smell and texture of freshly washed cotton sheets neatly tucked into the cushions where she slept when visiting, brought back a vivid sense of feeling safe, loved, and protected. She told me about sitting close to her grandmother as her grandmother brushed her long blond hair before tucking her into bed. We continued to talk about her new apartment and the possibility of creating a sacred space for herself similar to what she experienced at her grandmother's home. Christie became animated as she envisioned her new living space from this expanded perspective. I watched as the fear and anxiety about moving began to lift as she became more confident.

Transitions can be both scary and exciting for most of us. They cause us to leave what is familiar and venture into new territory. Though we may be looking forward to what's ahead, we can still feel uneasy. Transitions that are unwanted or painful can be even more anxiety producing. During these times we often look for stability. Creating a sanctuary at home where we feel safe is a powerful way to calm ourselves while moving through changes in life, helping to ease the transition.

Christie didn't have many possessions, but a new awareness of what sacred space meant to her helped reframe the move to her apartment in a positive light. Remembering first experiences of a safe haven is a wonderful starting point for exploring what we need in a sacred place and for making our current living environment responsive to our personal inclinations. Memories reveal important information about the types of spaces we are naturally drawn to when seeking sanctuary. Some of us may move toward wide, open expanses found on a rooftop, while others may need the security of an enclosed space hidden out of sight. The beauty is that we all have an intuitive knowing of what will feed our soul. Our memories can also give us concrete details about what a space looks like—the size, shape, color, views, light, and texture. Our childhood space may have been painted red, had a lot of light, had low ceilings, or been filled with soft pillows and blankets. By incorporating some of these details into our home, we reconnect with our childhood wisdom.

What we need in a sacred space may change over time, depending upon the season of life we are in, but we can always revisit the past to glean valuable insights into what will be supportive for us as we journey forward. Looking across the time line of our life beginning with our first experience of sacred space through the present moment, we can bring to mind the places that grounded us during critical crossroads or difficulties. A consistent theme or quality to our place of sanctuary may emerge - our personal and unique sense of what is Holy.

Original Experience of Sacred Space

Remembering our first encounter of finding or creating a special place for our self is a wonderful way to begin thinking about sacred space in our home. For many of us, this will have been in early childhood, but it could just as easily have been as a teenager, a young adult, or even recently. If nothing comes to mind, use this exercise to imagine a place where you would enjoy being. Take a few deep breaths and settle into a comfortable position.

When you have completed the exercise, write about your impressions from your sacred space, or using crayons, pastels, colored pencils, or watercolors, draw your special place. You may want to play with the colors and shapes that evoke the overall feeling or try using your non-dominant hand when drawing.

Meditation Exercise

In your mind's eye, I invite you to take a journey to your sacred place. Perhaps it is a secret hideout made from blankets pulled from the bed, or maybe it's somewhere you discovered high in the treetops overlooking the world. Maybe your sacred place is a secluded garden, the crevice of a rock near the ocean, a perch on a rooftop, or a hidden niche in a closet. Wherever your place is, imagine yourself there now. Remember it in as much detail as possible. Engage all your senses—sight, sound, touch, smell, and taste. What did the space look like? Was it dark and hidden, bright and open, colorful? How did it smell? Was the air musty or fresh or did it smell of old fabric? Was it a quiet place or were there sounds of water, creaky floors, or nearby traffic? How did the textures feel on your skin? Soft fabrics, cool earth, or rough tree limbs? What was the shape and size of your space? Large and expansive or small like a cocoon? What drew you there? How did you feel when you were there? Were you alone or with others? Take a few moments to just remember and linger in this place.

Nature

Nature is where we often experience sacred moments, hiking mountain trails, riding a horse in the tall grass of an open field, fishing along a stream, or sitting quietly while watching the sun set as the sky changes from orange to indigo blue. The vastness of the Grand Canyon, the massive breath and height of the sequoia trees in California and the wilderness in Yellowstone National Park are places that touch a place deep within us. Here we feel connected with our immediate surroundings and at the same time to something timeless and eternal. We can suspend our personal story line for a moment and become aware of God's vibrant presence in all things. Sacred places such as those found in nature provide a place to pause in the midst of our life and touch into an inner stillness within our soul. Such places resonate with our longing for mystery, wonder, and a sense of belonging—for something holy both within and around us.

I am reminded of a sacred place I encountered while on vacation with my family near Page, Arizona. Not long after my brother's death, my husband and I rented a boat and spent a week on Lake Powell with our young children and another family. I found having a little time alone each day maintained my sense of balance, particularly since the weight of grief still lingered in my heart. I had a morning ritual of arising with the glow of sunrise and the chatter of birds outside the houseboat. I'd slip out from the warmth of my sleeping bag and tiptoe past lumps of blankets and sleeping bags scattered on the floor, trying not to disturb the slumber of my fellow boat mates. Pulling on my life vest over a damp swimsuit, I'd untie the red kayak bobbing in the water behind the boat, settle into the seat, and push off toward the winding channels in Lake Powell.

The landscape here is strange and unnatural. Deep sandstone canyons are filled with water from the river that once flowed freely through their sheer walls but is now

calm splendor of my surroundings, and for a moment I felt like I was the only human alive - a part of the landscape itself, suspended in water, rock, and sky. As the week unfolded, I continued my morning explorations into the heart of the canyons. Sometimes I would pull my kayak ashore and lie on the beach, feeling the granular texture on my back and the warmth of the sun on my face, grateful for the solitude and the sense of wonder reawakened in my soul as I noticed my grief begin to lift.

It's this sense of wonder and rapport with our natural surroundings that restores our soul and heals wounds. Native Americans were particularly attuned to nature and understood the spiritual connection between themselves and the earth. The Blackfoot called the general power pervading nature natoji and trusted it to guide and assist their lives. They believed the Great Spirit manifested itself in the sun, moon, stars, morning mist, buffalo, beaver, eagle, or any living creature and sometimes objects. Physical form and spirit were seen as in-

contained by a dam. I was both repelled and intrigued by its eerie beauty—massive barren rocks, golden from the morning sunlight, contrasted with the vivid blue sky above. Abutting the rocks was a labyrinth of waterways that meandered into endless nooks and crannies. As I paddled into a secluded cove, I was captivated by the trinsically intertwined, not separate entities. Certain places were considered to have particular sacred qualities, such as Boynton Canyon in Sedona, Arizona, also known as Creation Canyon because of its masculine and feminine attributes. It was here that tribes from many different nations gathered for ceremonies and blessings, believing that the life force that animates all beings emanated from the mouth of the canyon.

Water, rocks, stone, natural lighting and vegetation connect a person with the natural setting. The shower pictured here extends into an outdoor garden.

Nature seems to have provided us with the need of interior silence.
We seek returning to a place of security, warmth and love.

~ Thomas Keating
Cistercian monk, abbot, & author

Bryce Canyon is another sacred place where erosion has shaped the malleable limestone into a magnificent array of spires, fins, and pinnacles known as hoodoos. These awe-inspiring sculptures resemble silhouettes of humans, shapes of animals, church steeples, and fortified walls. And if the light is just right, the face of a person will appear etched in the rocks. A legend of the Paiute Indians who inhabited the area for hundreds of years claims that the whimsical hoodoos are ancient Legend People whose spirits remain in the stones. The legend is worth taking to heart: we are intricately linked to our natural setting.

Being out doors recalibrates our internal compass and enlarges our perspective. It is hard to look at the expanse of the Grand Canyon, the massive redwood trees, or the towering beauty of Denali and not be touched by their enduring presence. They seem to remind us that we are only passing through, and despite our personal situations, there is something solid and graceful that remains and holds all things together. Our experiences in nature reassure us that all is well. Integrating earthy elements into our own home—such as lush green potted plants, water circulating through a fountain, wood floors, or a stone hearth and fireplace—forms a bond between our dwelling and the sacred qualities found in nature.

Tracey, an avid hiker and marketing executive, works from her home near the foothills of Boulder, Colorado. She used a delightful architectural detail to enhance the connection between her home and the landscape. To the side of her front door, a water chime dangles from the gutter attached to an overhanging roof above. When snow melts from the roof or a rain shower appears, a beautiful shimmer of water cascades down the chime into her potted plants below. It's a small feature that connects her home with the cycles of the earth.

Details that resonate with nature such as a water chime enhance a home.

Phil, an architect and painter, custom matched the color of his house with the backside of a Russian olive tree. He still gets requests and compliments from neighbors about the rich, earthy color. Another person collects rocks and shells from places he has traveled around the world. Some are displayed in a glass jar and others are scattered in trays and bowls throughout his home. They are a reminder of rafting down wild rapids, walking along the edge of the sea, or hiking on glaciers and they bring the essence of those places into his home. In that same vein, colors and textures found in nature can serve as inspiration for our own home. We may try creating a color and texture pallet from objects we find in nature grouping them according to season, time of day, or geographic location. For example: winter grasses, fall leaves, ocean landscape, or spring flowers.

Ancient Structures

Architecture is the reaching out for truth.

~ Louis Kahn
Architect

Spirituality is embedded in the history of humankind, and the sacred structures left behind are testament to an enduring quest to find meaning in life. Cathedrals, temples, shrines, and monuments such as the pyramids, the Parthenon, and Stonehenge are reminders of our desire to be connected to the mystery beyond ourselves. The shape and form of these structures flowed from each culture's technological skills and their understanding of the divine.

Some saw God as above, in heaven, and vertical elements of towers and spires reflected a reaching toward the heavens. Others understood the spiritual path as an inward journey, and caves, kivas and hermitages mirrored this inward movement. And like the Japanese Shinto religion, others saw God's spirit in all living things, and ornamentation of their shrines and temples included images of mountains, streams, the sun, moon, animals, and people.

Looking at these ancient structures, we can see three basic expressions of the spiritual journey: an upward movement, an inward movement, and an outward movement. God above is an awareness of something beyond us, an upward movement; God within is experienced through self-reflection and silence, an inward movement; and God in others is an outward expression that extends compassion to all living beings. The following examples capture the essence of each movement in physical forms found throughout the world.

Upward Movement ↑

Expressed in vertical structures
piercing through space

Stonehenge was constructed with monoliths, two large stone pillars capped with a large stone lintel. They were arranged in concentric circles with connecting pathways and were most likely part of a systemized ceremonial ritual that honored the cycles of the moon and sun.

The Ziggurat or temple tower was built with stairs for the God of the country to mount each night to return to heaven. Priests also stood on the top platform to pray to the Gods of night, stars, planets, and constellations.

The Pyramids of Gizah are associated with the sun god Re whose talisman was the ben-ben, a stone in the shape of a pyramid. Pharaohs may have believed that the spirit of Re resided in the ben-ben stone and that their divine spirits and bodies would be similarly preserved in the pyramid-shaped tombs.

Inward Movement

The Minaret or tower in the Great Masque of Samarra could be seen for miles around and was most likely used by the "muessin" who called people to prayer.

The Parthenon located at the top of a mound known as the Acropolis is a monument to the god Athena Parhenos and is a classic example of Greek temples. To reach the sacred building a procession of worshipers would have to walk from the lower level of the city up the steep hillside to the summit.

Standing in a cathedral one senses the largeness of God with towering vaulted ceilings held up by massive buttresses. The grand scale captures the power of God.

Expressed in spiraling structures and enclosed spaces

Buddhist cave sanctuaries were cut into rock cliffs and mirror the sense of moving into the depths of one's soul.

The dome shape of the Great Stupa in Sanchi without pointed roof lines invokes a quality of entering a womb.

The Kiva, buried in the ground, was the spiritual and ceremonial center of the Pueblo Indians. One had to climb down a wooden ladder to enter the space.

The Hermitage of St., Francis of Assisi is located on a hilltop and is a place of solitude.

Outward Movement →

Expressed in horizontal and open structures

The portico in St. Peter's square looks like two arms reaching out to gather in the citizens of Rome.

The grand courtyard of the Jewish temple or Islamic Mosque extended a welcome to people as they gathered to worship.

Gates signaled the entrance into a shrine or temple but they also mark the transition from the temple out into the surrounding community.

Drawings of the sun, moon, animals and landscapes found in sacred places express an outward focus, seeing God in all creation.

Though all three of these movements may be present in the same structure, one will dominate. The same is true for how we live out our spirituality. Paying attention to the expression that resonates with our core will guide us to spaces where we feel at home. We may even want to create our own symbol or find objects that capture the essence of the movement such as a nautilus shell that spirals inward or a tall potted plant that reaches upward. When our living spaces connect us with our personal spiritual path—inward, upward or outward—we experience a deepened sense of sanctuary.

Elizabeth, a middle-aged woman with two children, described her experience of the three spiritual movements and the physical structures that supported her. As a young girl she imagined God as being in heaven above her. Her family attended a church built in the Gothic Revival style, which suited her understanding of God because it was an upward-oriented structure. In the sanctuary, dark wood pews with deep green velvet cushions formed a semi-circle around the altar. Behind the altar was a podium and a large stone archway etched with angels that framed the choir loft with brass organ pipes behind, providing a dramatic backdrop. To the sides of the sanctuary were several stained-glass windows depicting biblical scenes crowned by a large rosette window above in hues of scarlet and deep blue. Even the ceiling was thoughtfully designed, a vaulted grid of plaster details accented with glass chandeliers suspended elegantly. It gave her the sense of being in the presence of a power greater than herself and that she was safe and protected, which felt comforting to her.

Moving into adulthood, she became more inward focused and was drawn to monasteries and retreat centers where solitude fed her soul. Guest rooms were furnished with a single bed, a small dresser, and a simple wooden desk with a lamp, and a white porcelain hand sink mounted to the wall. The stark simplicity of the room reflected the monastic lifestyle of prayer, poverty, and silence her hosts had chosen to live. It offered her a place to rest, to walk on the meandering trails surrounding the monastery, and to sort through the aftermath of a difficult divorce. Now as she enters the second season of her life, she notices a shift outward, wanting to contribute to her community, the health of the planet, and the well-being of others. Pathways and doors have become particularly meaningful for her, symbolic of moving out into the world. Walking the labyrinth is a powerful physical experience that parallels her spiritual path of moving inward toward the center of the circle, then outward toward community.

Our personality, experiences, and culture all influence our spirituality. Though all three movements in the spiritual journey are valid, we will often lean toward one or another depending upon where we are in our life. The movements do not follow a progression or order, and one is not superior to the other; each has a place and purpose in deepening our understanding of God's presence. It is a circular dynamic that allows for flexibility and responsiveness to our needs. Knowing where we are on this continuum is helpful information that allows us to find or create the kind of personal spaces that are most supportive. The upward movement might be expressed with a vaulted ceiling, tall windows, or other vertical details such as a floor lamp, candles, or a stairway. Bathtubs, doorways, low ceilings, and curves, invite us inward while horizontal lines found in long tables, pathways, halls, or artwork capture the essence of the outward movement.

Vaulted ceilings, ascending stairways, arched windows or doors, and other vertical details capture the essence of the upward movement.

The bed niche with a low ceiling above it and the deep hot tub invite an inward movement.

The long, horizontal table and meandering pathway seem to reach outwards.

Body Wisdom

Our first experience of life is not a merely visual one of knowing ourselves through other people's responses. But this experience of ourselves is primarily felt in the body. It's not heard or seen or thought. It is felt. That's original knowing.

~ Morris Berman
Author & academic

Another source of intuitive wisdom comes through our five senses: seeing, hearing, touching, tasting, and smelling. Body wisdom. This is a non-verbal knowing that understands and has access to the Holy in a way that our mind and emotions cannot. Our body responds to the tangible world surrounding it, taking in subtle information that our mind may not notice. We aren't usually conscious of it, but our senses are constantly assimilating information from the environment, registering and responding to temperature, odors, lighting, background noises, facial expressions, and tone of voice. Unlike our mind that can wander to the past or fret about the future,

our body dwells in the present moment, and this is where sacred encounters are possible. When we focus our attention on our senses, we allow our body to ground us in the present and open ourselves up to a wisdom and guidance that is different from our thinking mind. Our senses are a wonderful tool, and by simply taking a few deep breaths or intently listening to the sounds surrounding us we can re-engage our physicality. Many of us have had an experience of pondering an important decision in our life and considering all the practical options only to have a "gut feeling" that conflicted with our rational thought process. Perhaps our body was responding to physical cues we couldn't name. This was the case for Jessica who tried listening to her body to get clarity concerning a decision she needed to make.

During one of our spiritual-direction sessions, Jessica shared her struggle about an invitation to participate in an advocacy group she had a passion for. She could see the pros and cons of the situation but couldn't seem to land on a decision that felt right. I asked her to sit quietly and imagine saying yes to joining the group. At the same time I asked her to notice what she felt in her body. I then asked her to do the same exercise but consider not joining the group. She immediately had her answer. When she thought about participating, her chest and shoulders tightened up; when she thought of saying no to the invitation, it was like a weight had been lifted. Sometimes the signals aren't so obvious, but with practice we can begin to discern the insights our body has to offer.

Along with offering guidance, our body provides a link to our personal history. Research suggests that a person's sense of smell is the strongest factor in triggering old memories. Diesel fuel may conjure up fond memories of sitting on a tractor beside one's father for example, while the smell of horses in the barn may bring a familiar sense of comfort for another. Our five senses register pleasure or dis-

comfort very quickly, and long before we had the cognitive skills to articulate these experiences in thoughts or words, our body understood their meaning. We are so connected with the physical environment that natural light increases our concentration level and listening to classical music stimulates the immune system and accelerates the healing process. Looking to the home, we can use our five senses to decipher what makes a space feel good. Light, temperature, sound, and smell all have an impact on how we feel in a room.

Jonathan, a self-employed businessman, works from his home and is strongly affected by his environment. He is particularly sensitive to temperature and prefers warm climates where pain from an old injury is lessened. Unfortunately, he and his family live in a place where the weather changes with the seasons and winters can become quite cold. The discomfort he experiences during cold spells affects not only his body but his moods as well. Whether it's too hot or too cold, the temperature of a room matters. For Jonathan, the thermostat became a battleground as he constantly increased the heat only to have his wife lower it again. Putting his office on a separate heating zone and purchasing an electric blanket with dual controls has helped, but he has also chosen to spend several weeks each winter in a warmer climate to alleviate some of the stress caused by cold temperatures.

Sally, on the other hand, is a young woman who has a highly tuned sense of smell. Perfumes, air-fresheners, and other fragrances trigger migraine headaches, so she chooses to

The sound of water, the smell of incense, the soft texture of velvet on our skin are a few ways our senses connect us to our dwelling.

use unscented detergents, cleaners, and deodorants to create a comfortable environment for herself. For someone else, the fresh smell of fabric softener on newly laundered sheets may be connected with a sense of cleanliness and positive feelings. Most of us are not as sensitive as Sally, but cigarette smoke, odors from pets, or gas fumes from the garage can be just as irritating to us as perfume is to her. Along with temperature and our sense of smell, the sounds in and around our home affect us as well. My husband loves to turn up the stereo when he comes home from work because loud music energizes his spirit, and he is naturally drawn to activity. In contrast, I am happiest in a quiet space and can feel my whole body relax into silence but become agitated in a room with a lot of noise.

We all have varying degrees of tolerance for light, sound, temperature, fragrance, color, and texture. These can be a source of conflict or an opportunity to find a balance that honors each person's sensitivities. As we are going about our day, we can cultivate a habit of checking in with our body from time-to-time. What is our first reaction when walking into the grocery store, the coffee shop, or a doctor's office? Does the aroma of brewing coffee entice us, are we drawn to the colorful produce department, or does the hum of a dentist drill send shivers down our spine? Becoming aware of our preferences and the preferences of those living with us is important because to feel relaxed and secure in our home, our home must be responsive to our body. The gift of physicality is that it allows us to experience the Holy in a tangible way.

Like a mirror to the soul, our home often reflects what's happening internally for us as well. We can use this awareness to make adjustments in our environment that facilitate changes we'd like to experience within. For example, if I am trying to simplify my life and want to slow down a bit, I might consider eliminating extraneous sounds by turning off the TV at night and listening to instrumental music instead. If my home feels disorganized, I might ask myself what feels out of control in my life right now. Sorting through the pile of mail stacked on the desk may bring the clarity I'm seeking. By paying attention to our body and the concrete qualities of our living space, we have a compass for creating environments that resonate with both our body and spirit.

An intuitive understanding of sacred space is something we all possess, whether we tap into it in nature, through history or early childhood experiences, or by paying attention to what feels good to our body. No one can tell us what our own sacred space is; we each understand it for ourselves. The following chapters offer guidance for accessing this inner knowing and tools to help articulate what is often hard to put into words.

Tuning into Your Body

Becoming more aware of our five senses helps us feel connected to our physical surroundings. In the following exercise you will become attuned to your body. Begin by finding a comfortable place to sit with a view out a window if possible. Read through the exercise once, then read it again slowly, pausing between segments. If you have time, sit for a few minutes before getting up.

The soft texture of the fur throw adds a sense of warmth and comfort to this bedroom.

Meditation Exercise

Close your eyes and take three deep breaths. Focus your attention on your hearing. Notice the sounds outside the window: maybe the rumble of distant traffic, wind blowing through trees, birds chirping. Try to identify as many sounds as possible. Now bring your attention inside the room. What do you hear? Creaking floorboards, the hum of a refrigerator, music from the radio? Notice your breath as you breathe in and out. Try listening inside your body. Can you hear your pulse?

Keeping your eyes closed, feel the weight of your body as you sit on a chair, a couch, or the floor. Is the surface soft, hard, warm? Adjust yourself until you feel comfortable. What textures are touching your skin? Notice how they feel. Beginning with your feet, relax your muscles as you move your attention up your body, moving from your toes to your ankles, calves, thighs, hips, abdomen, arms, shoulder, neck, jaw, eyes, and forehead. Now feel your breath as it moves in through your nose and into your lungs—feel your chest expand and contract—feel your heart beating in your chest.

Take a moment to notice the smells in the room and identify as many as possible. Which are familiar? Which are appealing? Are there any unpleasant odors? Open your eyes and gaze out the window or in the distance in the room. Pay attention to the quality of light and the colors. Is there an object you are drawn to? Let your eyes settle there as you notice the shape, color, and details that are visually compelling. Close your eyes one last time. Do a brief scan of your body focusing on your sense of sound, touch, smell, and sight. Try doing this throughout the day.

Exercises

1. Write a definition of what sacred space means to you or make a list of words that describe its characteristics. The words below will help you get started.

   secret quiet mysterious open enclosed soft musty light hidden safe protected dark calm serene earthy cozy wild peaceful majestic

2. Write about how you have experienced each of the three movements of the spiritual path: upward, inward, and outward. Which is most active in your life now and why? Do elements in your home match your interior experience?

3. Take an inventory of your senses. On a piece of paper, make seven columns. Label the columns as follows: sounds, textures/surfaces, temperatures, smells, light, color/shape, taste.

Under each column, write down things you like—for example, sounds of a fire crackling, soft fuzzy blankets, cool night air, onions and garlic sauteing, morning sunlight, earth tones, clean lines, sour fruit. Give yourself plenty of room to add to your list as new ideas come to mind. On a separate piece of paper, make the same columns as above but on this sheet keep track of what you don't like. You can make your own categories as well. How does your list differ from the list of someone you live with?

Notes

Rules of Thumb

• Remember your early encounters of sacred space and as many physical details as possible. These places and spaces reveal what's important to you and can inspire you as you create a sacred home.

• Adding plants, stones, seashells, or other items found outdoors to your home is a simple way to ground it to the earth and the sacred qualities found in nature. Green plants, either real or silk, are especially important to include on the interior because they enliven a space.

• Keep in mind your five senses. The soothing sound of a water fountain, the fresh smell of flowers, or the smooth touch of leather can elicit a positive connection with your home.

• Pay attention to the acoustics in your home. Does sound travel from the public areas to the private spaces that you prefer were quiet? The sound of water from a small fountain or the quiet hum of a fan can mask unwanted noise.

• The three movements of the spiritual journey—inward, upward, and outward—are expressed in physical forms. Add objects to your home that reflect your personal inclination.

• Trust your innate ability to recognize and create sacred space.

Chapter 2

The Tabernacle as Archetype for Sacred Space

All the most powerful ideas in history go back to archetypes.

~ Carl G. Jung
Psychiatrist, analytical psychologist, & writer

Archetypes

Buildings and spaces that feel good to us usually have a unifying pattern or theme that holds them together, whether it's a central courtyard, a linear axis, or a symmetrical layout. I was curious if such a pattern could be found in historic sacred spaces. What I discovered was an ancient sanctuary called the Tabernacle, an elaborate desert tent used for worship that embodied a clear pattern for creating sacred space. I was drawn to this particular structure because of its simplicity of design that was both straightforward and uncomplicated. The ease of relating the patterns found there to a home environment made it appealing to use as a template for sacred space. Though it is not the only model, it has an archetypal quality to it that is easy to use and remember.

Archetypes are patterns that have existed throughout time. They resonate with our core being or essence, helping us articulate what makes a place feel sacred.

Archetypes come in many forms: common personality types, repeated shapes and forms of structures, rhythms of the seasons, the cycles of the sun and the moon, the cadence of an ocean wave and even the steady beating of our heart. Physical archetypes—such as the dome, the cube, and the pyramid—have appeared in many cultures around the world and have been used repeatedly throughout history. Archetypes are patterns that speak a language deeper than words—just as symbols, poetry, and great art do—and they feel familiar. They're a link between our ancestors and us, and also a link between human beings and the eternal qualities of God. If we pay attention, archetypes help us be in sync with the design of the universe, and when our homes are aligned with this ancient wisdom we encounter a sense of sanctuary in the places we dwell.

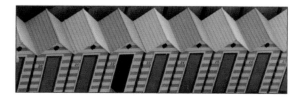

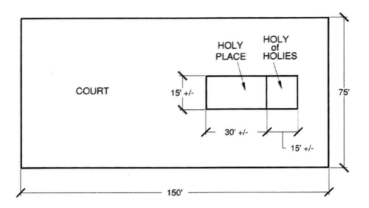

COURT

HOLY PLACE

HOLY of HOLIES

15' +/-

75'

30' +/-

15' +/-

150'

Layout of the Tabernacle depicting three main spaces:
Public, Private and Intimate

The Pattern of Three

One of the foundational archetypes reflected in the Tabernacle is a numeric pattern of three, a number associated with the Divine, the Great Spirit, God, or the Source of Life. Its structure consisted of three major spaces: the Court, the Holy Place, and the Holy of Holies. Similarly, Buddhist temples consist of three essential buildings: the pagoda, the great hall, and the monastic study hall. The Great Pyramids of Egypt are grouped in threes, and the three foundations of the Tao are heaven, earth, and man. In the Christian tradition, God is expressed in the triad of Father, Son, and Holy Spirit. If we understand how the pattern of three works, we can integrate it into our homes and into our lives, creating beautiful spaces that have a sacred rhythm and balance. The archetype, as expressed in the Jewish Tabernacle, provides the template we need.

The Tabernacle, a tent used for worship by the nomadic Jewish herdsmen, was divided into three spaces that included a large, open-aired, public area known as the Court, a quiet, enclosed private space called the Holy Place, and an intimate room in complete darkness and silence that was the Holy of Holies. Each space expressed different aspects of the sacred experience and enhanced one another. Rituals tied the three spaces together as a progression of movement flowed inward toward the stillness of the Holy of Holies then back out to the boisterous court. Like the inhalation and exhalation of breath, this movement back and forth between the three spaces kept the Tabernacle alive—a living, breathing sanctuary—breathing in toward silence, exhaling into community.

The fluid motion between the three spaces encompassed multiple layers of sensory experiences. Changes in the size, shape, lighting, temperature, color, and texture of each area reflects the dynamic and varied experiences of God. Though the high priest was the only person allowed in the inner sanctum of the Holy of Holies, the stark contrast between the Court and the Holy of Holies helped prepare him for an encounter with God. Sunlight shifted to candlelight inside the tent and then to total darkness within the Holy of Holies. The cacophony of animals and people gathered in the Court faded into whispers within the Holy Place and then into silence. Heat from the desert sun softened in the cool, musty shade of the tent.

Court	Holy Place	Holy of Holies
Public	Private	Intimate
Large	Medium	Small
Light	Shadow	Darkness
Loud	Quiet	Silent
Action	Stillness	Contemplation
Color	Subtle Hues	Black
Hot	Warm	Cool
Community	Family	Individual

The Flow of Movement between Spaces

Each space had its own mood, moving from vibrant energy to subtle calmness. The priest would have felt the scorching desert heat upon his skin as he mingled among a crowd of people and animals. Slowly, he would have moved into a shaded and fragrant candle-lit room where a few priests tended an altar of incense before entering into the cool stillness in the depths of the tent. The Holy Place would have also served as a transition area when the priest emerged from the sacred darkness before opening the curtain into the bright light of the Court where a large gathering of people awaited him, ready to hear the blessing he had received from God. The continual movement between communion with others and communion with the Holy infused the Tabernacle with life.

Valerie—a writer, artist, and therapist—has created a home with rich layers of sensory experiences that are similar to those of the Tabernacle. The outdoor areas of her home are filled with gardens, patios, and porches, and like the Court in the Tabernacle they invite a person to draw near. The Holy Places where she and her daughters enjoy being together tend to be in the kitchen, the family room, and the breakfast nook where playful colors and decorative fabrics enliven the space. Each person has a space to call her own with details that reflect her personality. For the girls it is their room, and for Valerie, her Holy of Holies is her art studio.

Every room in Valerie's home offers sensory delights and conveys subtle changes in atmosphere. On the exterior of her home, the covered porches with their deep overhangs offer a shady respite from the afternoon heat during summer days when she tends her gardens where herbs and flowers sweeten the air with their perfume. Coming into the house is like moving into the Holy Place of the Tabernacle, where window seats tucked along the edges of the family room are a perfect place to snuggle up with a book and enjoy the warmth of sunlight streaming through the window on a winter day or listen to the crackling fire in the nearby stone fireplace. When she's cooking in the kitchen, the smooth sounds of Miles Davis play in the background while flickers of candlelight dance across deep red walls.

These window seats allow for a cozy setting within the larger space of the family room.

Her art studio is where she goes when she needs time to re-center. Here she engages her body, mind, and spirit in painting canvases, an activity that feeds her soul. Homes that have a rich pallet of sensory encounters resonate with our spiritual journey that also has many layers and dimensions varying from being open and vibrant to places that are dark and silent. It feels

good when our surroundings match our interior terrain and have the capacity to hold an array of moods.

The temple or sanctuary is often used as a metaphor for our interior world. In the New Testament of the Bible (1 Corinthians 3:16), Paul writes in a letter to the Corinthians, "Don't you know your body is the temple of God where the spirit dwells?" The archetypes that apply to the physical realm also shape the spiritual realm. The wisdom and guidance we find in the Tabernacle influence both our internal and external worlds. Like the high priest who entered the darkness of the Holy of Holies to encounter God, we need times of solitude and communion with spirit. It was from this direct contact with the Holy Mystery that the priest was able to return to the outer court to bless the people. Our activities can be sustained only if we have times for just being. On the other hand, if we were to spend all our time in the Holy of Holies, the community would miss out on receiving our gifts, and our spiritual life would stagnate. Depending on our personality, we will have a propensity toward one of the three spaces, but the rhythm of the Tabernacle invites us to explore all three areas. If we are naturally extroverts, moving toward stillness can feel challenging. If we're introverted, moving out of the comfort of the Holy of Holies into action may be our growing edge. Our physical surroundings can support the movement within our interior temple. For example, a quiet space void of distractions encourages interior stillness, while a large open area lends itself to coming together with others. For our lives and our dwelling to feel sacred, all three spaces need to be available so we can move freely between them. Each place has a purpose and contributes to a sense of wholeness. Applying this archetypal pattern to our living environment begins by identifying the spaces in our homes that are similar to those found in the Tabernacle.

The Public Space of the Court

The Court, or public space, was a large outdoor area where families, animals, and priests gathered in preparation for making an offering to God. A cacophony of sounds and smells filled the air. Cattle, sheep, goats, and a variety of birds were available to purchase to offer as sacrifice. The wail of the animals, the smoke from the burning altar, and the prayers of the people all mingled together. The Court was quite literally the edge between the ordinary lives of the Israelites and what they held as sacred. They came together in a large community in the Court to socialize and worship God. Here they were welcomed into a sacred place and received a blessing from the priest before they returned to their daily routines and work. In our homes, the spaces similar to the Court include entrances, front porches, and front yards that border the streets and lanes surrounding our dwelling in the community where we live. They provide a segue between the bustling world outside and the privacy within our home. It is the place where we invite people to enter inside.

Porches, gates, courtyards and plants soften the transition between the public street and the privacy of our home.

Emma, a freelance marketing consultant, works from her home and is constantly coming and going. After attending a workshop about sacred space, she began to notice how she enters her home. She rarely uses the front door and almost always parks her car in her garage and then walks through the laundry room into the kitchen. While her front patio is welcoming to others, her garage entrance felt dismal. She didn't have a lot of financial resources to make major changes, but she came up with a simple yet creative solution to her entry problem. First, she repainted the laundry room a warm yellow. Then she hung a favorite painting on the blank wall above the washing machine where she could see it every time she walked through the door. Pondering the door between the garage and laundry room, she decided to paint it a bright color to cheer her up when she came home. Over the top of the door in the garage she hung a *Welcome Home* sign. On the other side she painted the word *Blessings* so she would see it every time she left home.

Feeling welcomed is particularly important when we enter a home for the first time. Will, a financial advisor, describes his positive experience when arriving at a vacation home in Hawaii. Surrounding the house was a thick rock privacy wall with stucco pillars and a handcrafted wood door that marked the entrance and opened into a beautiful courtyard. Lush tropical plants, a small waterfall carved into lava rock, and a guest cottage adjacent to the house contributed to a sense of being embraced, and he felt immediately at ease. It was a wonderful transition from the local street into the ambiance of the home. As we enter our own home we can pay particular attention to the transition between the street and the front door, noticing if it feels welcoming. If bushes or overhanging tree limbs block the view to our front door or its unclear where it is located, a sense of ambiguity will cause resistance to entering further. On the other hand, when we have a clear view of the entrance and it feels inviting, we naturally want to move toward it.

This wooden gate opens to a welcoming courtyard.

Large front porches have an allure that make them an ideal portal into the privacy of a home, and like the Court they are semi-enclosed outdoor spaces that border the edges of society. Jill, who had recently purchased horse property, wanted to include a porch in the design of her new home because she liked the way they looked and felt. Upon further reflection, she realized what she enjoyed about porches was the community aspect of them. They reminded her of her childhood in the South where neighbors lingered on their porches and greeted one another

when passing by. To her a porch was a welcoming space where she could sit outside without being completely exposed to the elements and chat with fellow horse owners in an informal setting. How we enter our home sets the tone for what lays ahead.

As a mirror to our soul, the interior court is the interface between our private and public lives, the place we engage with the broader community. For those of us who are more private, venturing into the public arena may seem frightening, but to keep a vibrant spiritual life we need to risk ourselves; it allows areas in our life to grow that need the context of a larger group to develop into fullness. Teresa is a woman who was willing to overcome her fears and move into the public light. She is a talented yet shy writer whose stories are both poignant and humorous. Her writing describes the joys and trials of everyday life, from raising children, to watching a dear friend die of cancer to the serendipity of almost running into some-one's loose pet mink while driving on the back roads of Tennessee. Her stories almost always make the reader laugh and often cry, but she only shared them with a few fellow writers and family. The idea of sending her work to a publisher felt intimidating, yet many people were missing out on her insights and humor because she was afraid her writing wasn't good enough. With encouragement from friends, Teresa submitted a story to a local public radio station. She was invited to read it on the air, and many listeners called to say how touched they were by her words. We might examine our own experience with public venues, perhaps as a teacher or speaker or a performer of some kind. We can notice if we were energized by our experience or if we had to draw on our reserves to show up, if we felt at home or a bit nervous. Either way, the court is where we share our talent, our insights, and our knowledge with others.

The Private Space of the Holy Place

Crossing the threshold from the Court into the private area of the Tabernacle, priests entered a candle-lit room within the tent that was called the Holy Place. Unlike the outer court, it was an enclosed space, fragrant with incense. Only a select group of priests were allowed into this private space where they tended the altar and practiced devotions and rituals that honored their God. A wooden table with bread offerings stood on one side and golden candelabra on the other. At the center of the room was an altar where incense was burned, symbolizing their prayers ascending to the heavens. Akin to the Holy Place, the private spaces in our home are places where we gather together with family and friends to share our personal stories. Moving beyond the welcome of the Court, we come together to nurture our relationships, and this in turn sustains the holy place within our being. Dining rooms, kitchens, family rooms, patios, and gardens provide a space for these encounters.

My home has a covered back deck with soft lounge furniture, glass side tables, candles, lamps, and hanging plants. The secluded outdoor setting invites impromptu gatherings of friends and neighbors where we linger over a cup of coffee or a glass of wine and share the news of our children, our work, and our hearts. Paying attention to the places where we naturally gravitate for conversation is one way to bring awareness to how this archetypal pattern is active in our home. It can also be worthwhile noting which rooms are rarely used in our home. A formal living room may have become dead space as guests mingle in the kitchen. Maybe there is an activity we enjoy doing with others that can transform it into a vibrant space again.

A covered porch offers a comfortable place to gather with family and friends.

Josh is a poet and teacher whose creative juices are fueled by sharing his craft with others. To keep his writing fresh, he hosts a gathering of writers and poets once a month to read aloud their most recent work. This select group of creative souls, similar to the priests in the Tabernacle, shares a common passion. Large plush pillows strewn on the floor in the family room along with a soft overstuffed couch provide the perfect setting for them to relax as they listen to each other's lilting voices fill the space. Josh says these monthly get-togethers have become an important part of his life, and he can't imagine ending them. His family room takes on a sacred quality whenever the group gathers, and each person leaves feeling refreshed at the end of the evening.

Similarly, Kevin has met with a small group of men for over twenty years. They began by meeting at a coffee shop twice a month to talk about life, their work, and their families or to discuss a book they were reading together. Eventually they gravi-tated to the loft apartment of a friend who lived in the center of town. The spacious balcony overlooking the street below has a circular gas fireplace with several lounge chairs and small tables surrounding it. Views of the city lights and the hillside in the distance provide a beautiful backdrop for the group when they come together in the private alcove tucked above the bustling retail shops below.

When we join others on a retreat, sit in a small circle of friends to pray, listen and laugh with those we love, we sense a bond that knits our hearts together. This is the holy place within our selves that resonates with the holy place in others and longs to be in communion. We can risk letting down our guard and be ourselves. If we are not ready to share our thoughts with the larger community, we can build our confidence in the sacred circle of those who know us well. Paying attention to the important people in our lives and cultivating these relationships strengthens the holy place in our spirit.

Tending the holy place within can sometimes be challenging in the midst of busy lives where we are distracted by the many tasks that need to be addressed. Too often we take for granted those closest to us or simply slip into routines that lack meaningful connection. Jennifer, a paralegal and mother of three, began feeling out of touch with her family as her children became more involved in school activities. Juggling her children's schedules and her work became more complicated, and often her only contact with her children was driving them to an event or practice. There was rarely an evening when everyone was home at the same time, and she missed the days of sharing a meal together where she caught up on the details of each child's day and sensed the tenor of his or her mood. In an effort to re-establish a family connection, Jennifer instituted a "family night" once a week. Each family member made it a priority to set the evening aside to eat dinner together and play games or watch a movie. It wasn't always easy to carve out time to spend together, but her family came to savor these special evenings. As adults her children still come to her home on a regular basis for "family night."

Having a delightful place in our home where we can share a meal with family and friends connects us with our dwelling.

Quiet spaces in our home, invite stillness within.

The Intimate Space of the Holy of Holies

Behind a curtain four inches thick, deep within the Tabernacle, was the Holy of Holies. Here the most precious relics of the Jewish people were stored in complete darkness in an earthy room with a cool sand floor. Only the high priest was allowed into the Holy of Holies to encounter God's presence. A string was tied around his ankle to pull him out if he became overwhelmed by the experience and passed out or died. The most intimate areas of our home, like the Holy of Holies, are the places where we reconnect with what brings meaning to our life. So often the still small voice within our soul gets drowned out by the demands of life. Few things in our culture support our need for serenity, our need to take time to be still and listen; yet serenity is essential for our well-being. Sitting rooms, bedrooms, studies, art studios, wood shops, and meditation rooms provide physical space for us to rekindle our passions and connection with God's spirit. Sometimes we have to be creative to find space for our personal Holy of Holies—it's easy to overlook.

Finding a place to do what we love seasons our home with joy.

Dee, who lives on a farm, created a personal Holy of Holies by converting a small wood-framed bunkhouse on her property into a weaving studio. A loom and wood stove along with colorful spools of yarn fill the rectangular room and provide a place for her to meditate as she relaxes into the steady motion of weaving. Having a space of our own doesn't have to mean taking over an entire room. A nook under the stairway or a chair tucked into a corner of a room is perfect.

Having a place to recharge was important to Dan, a youth minister who managed a small staff and several volunteers. The demands of being a companion to teenagers, with all their angst and emotional drama, was draining him and fellow workers. He had read a story about Julia of Norwich, a saint from the late 1300's, who lived in a room attached to the church called the "anchor hold." This simple enclosure had a small window known as a "squint" that opened into the church and another that opened into the street. When the shutters were open to the street, Julia would converse with those seeking guidance or prayer. Through the other window she could watch and hear the church service. The purpose of the anchor hold was to provide a place to be completely open to God in prayer without distractions, much like the Holy of Holies.

Dan wanted to create a place like the anchor hold where his staff and volunteers could take a break, be still, and open themselves to a higher wisdom.

A tool shed attached to the back of the century-old home where his office was located seemed like the perfect place to create this space. A small window in the shed looked out over a hay field, and a single light bulb hung from the ceiling. The dirt floor was leveled and compacted. He poured a concrete slab over the dirt and found some carpet remnants to place on top. A small kneeler was donated to the project as well as some floor pillows, candles, and a space heater. At first the members of his staff were reluctant to take time for themselves, but eventually the anchor hold became an integral part of their ministry.

Our spirit craves solitude, yet we give it up so easily when life's demands keep us busy. The irony is that when we don't take time for ourselves, we end up feeling fatigued, drained, and less effective in facing the tasks at hand. Allowing moments of stillness actually increases our energy which helps us take care of what needs to be done. In the story of the Tabernacle, the high priest was able to bless the congregation only after spending time in the Holy of Holies where he was renewed by the presence of God. It is here we find the resources and wisdom we need. This doesn't need to be a major shift in our lifestyle. Even a few minutes a day can recharge our batteries.

Finding the Right Balance

The balance created among the public, private, and intimate areas of the Tabernacle enhanced its sacredness. Without all three spaces the Tabernacle would be incomplete. The contrast of the experiences within the three areas added depth and character to the Tabernacle. Moving between the three spaces allowed for varied and complex encounters, from the vibrant outer Court to the seclusion of the Holy of Holies. The same is true for our homes. When our home welcomes us, when it has places where we connect with those we love and also places that allow for solitude and stillness, it will feel like a sanctuary. Finding the right balance between the three spaces will be unique to each of us. Depending on our personality and the personalities of the people living with us, we will emphasize one of the areas in our home. Knowing which of the three areas is most important to us is valuable information. A social person may need a lot of square footage devoted to the public area in the home, while an artist might need a large studio to foster personal creativity. The balance between the public, private, and intimate spaces in our home will be determined by our personal needs and values.

One couple I worked with discovered that what they needed in a home had changed after their children had grown. Emily and Bill had recently become empty nesters and wanted to incorporate the concepts of Sacred Space in their search for a new home. They narrowed their selection to three houses but couldn't make a final decision. One had fallen in love with a house, while the other partner was just mildly interested and vice versa. They had come to an impasse. Each felt they had to either give up their dream house to live in a place they weren't excited about or live with an unhappy partner. When they considered the three main areas of a home—public, private, and intimate—they were able to see clearly why they couldn't agree on a home. Emily valued having friends and neighbors over for dinner and wanted a large, open gathering area for entertaining while Bill longed for a quiet study for reading and writing now that the children were grown. Both wanted to downsize to simplify their lives. None of the houses they were considering accommodated each person's needs. Armed with this new information, they were able to find a home they both loved, a smaller home with an open main level and a secluded loft above, a home that met their individual needs but also reflected their values as a couple.

Just as Emily and Bill were able to find a home that fit their needs, the pattern of three as expressed in the Tabernacle offers a guide for creating a sense of sacredness in our living spaces. Sacred living invites us to move between public, private, and intimate activities. All aspects of the human experience are embraced within the Tabernacle and reflected in its structure. The continuum of moods and emotions that accompanies the spiritual path are supported and welcomed: light, dark, shadow, loud, quiet, soft, rough, smooth, hot, cold, sweet fragrances, and strong smells. Personal contemplation, community gatherings, and everything in between has a place. The Tabernacle invites us to include a full range of experiences in our living spaces and in our interior spaces as well. Whether we are drawn to public space, private space, or intimate space, we can create a balance between the three that nurtures our well-being.

Exercises

1. On a sheet of paper, make three columns and label them Public, Private, and Intimate (or Court, Holy Place, and Holy of Holies). List each room, space, or area in your home (both indoors and outdoors) in the column that best describes it. Some rooms or spaces may be in more than one category.

2. Draw a large circle. Divide the circle into three wedges that represent the public, private, and intimate spaces in your home. If your home has mostly public areas, then that piece of the circle will be the largest. Give each category a color—for example, green for private areas, red for public, and purple for intimate. List the activities that happen there, such as watching TV, cooking, or reading. Now draw another circle and divide it into segments that represent your ideal balance between the three areas. How do the two circles compare?

3. Does the balance between public, private, and intimate spaces in your home seem lopsided? If so, what types of spaces would you need to add or subtract for a better balance?

Notes

Rules of Thumb

• A home will feel sacred when there is a balance between public, private, and intimate spaces that reflect your personality and the activities that are important to you.

•Take the same care to welcome yourself home as you take to welcome guests into your home. Try placing a small shelf or table near the door you use on a regular basis to drop keys, newspapers, or mail. Add an outlet for phone chargers and a table lamp if possible. These small conveniences make a big difference in how you feel when entering your home.

• Consider adding artwork near the entrance where guest arrive and also where you enter your home as well.

• Private sitting areas can be as simple as a window seat with plush pillows or chairs by a small fireplace. A 9'x 9' room will accommodate two overstuffed chairs and a small table nicely.

• Remember to find a place in your home you can call your own, a place where you can recharge. Personal space in a home is a counterbalance to the community spaces.

Chapter 3

A Closer Look at the Holy of Holies

You must have a room or a certain hour of the day or so where you do not know what is in the morning paper. A place where you can simply experience and bring forth what you are and what you might be. At first you may think nothing's happening. But if you have a sacred space and take advantage of it and use it everyday, something will happen.

~ Joseph Campbell
American Mythologist, writer, & lecturer.

An Invitation to Stillness

The Tabernacle, located in the center of the Israelites' camp, had a sense of enchantment about it and was a visual reminder of their connection to something larger than themselves. Like a church in the center of town, or the morning call to prayer in Islamic cities, it served as a respite from the day-to-day grind of survival in what were often harsh conditions. Lush fabrics, fragrances, and rituals invited rest and rejuvenation for the soul. As children, my brother, sister, and I created our own version of a sacred tent. Pulling blankets and pillows from our beds, we headed to the basement playroom of our two-story Midwestern home. Here we constructed a tent that included a long dark tunnel we crawled through to reach the main room whose curtain would only be lifted with the secret password. Flashlights lit our tent made from the quilts just as the candelabra lit the Jewish tent made from animal skins. Like the Tabernacle that housed sacred relics, our tent protected our most precious items: an Indian-head nickel, a Raggedy Ann doll, a dime-store diamond ring, bubble gum, and a baseball card of our favorite St. Louis Cardinal, Bob Gibson. The door to our tent transported us into a world full of wonder and mystery.

We need places where we reconnect with the mystery in life, places of retreat, relaxation, and stillness that balance the routine and often hectic pace of daily living. Gary, a marriage and family therapist and outdoor enthusiast, takes an annual trek to the hot mineral springs in Ojo Caliente, New Mexico. He has discovered that changing up his normal routine with a trip to the high dessert is essential for living a balanced and vibrant life. Like the hot water that bubbles up through the layers of the earth, he feels his own creative energy rise to the surface as he soaks in the soothing waters.

The springs have drawn travelers for centuries, and legends abound of their healing powers. Native Americans believed Mother

Earth offered the mineral pools as a way to restore those who lingered in her liquid embrace. Gary says he leaves the hot springs feeling peaceful and realigned with his inner truth. He strongly advocates that his clients take a break from old patterns and routines to go someplace intriguing as a way to rekindle wonder and intimacy in their relationships. Finding a place for quiet moments in our home is important too. We might pause for a few minutes to soak in the warm water of a hot tub on the back patio while gazing at the stars above, or add bath salts to the tub and candlelight to our bathroom to create a place for relaxation and stillness.

When a home contains these kinds of spaces, it offers a centering point that nourishes a sense of well-being and restores our vigor for life. One of my clients, an avid weekend climber and successful business man, lit up when I suggested a climbing wall be added to the list of items to be included in the remodel his home. He was delighted with the idea and de-cided to build it. In our weekly meetings with the contractor, he exuded a childlike enthusiasm whenever the details of his climbing wall, an adult version of a playground, were discussed. With the remodel complete, he rises early in the morning before heading into the office. Pulling on his harness, he clips him self into a safety rope and reaches toward a hand hold or foothold. As he angles and stretches his body across the multi-faceted wall, he is consumed with the joy of climbing.

The climbing wall in this home is a place of pure enjoyment.

Mary, on the other hand, is a passionate reader and budding writer. She found a way to restore the pleasure of unstructured time into her life by creating a place to linger with her books. She converted a large clothes closet into a mini-library by removing the double doors and adding shelves for her novels and first edition books. It's a place where she shifts gears and gets lost in stories that take her mind far away to captivating places. It allows her to view her life from an expanded perspective and often helps her reframe particular circumstances that have been difficult for her. This is what sacred space does. It restores a sense of balance in our life where we can experience wonder, joy, and delight. Taking a break from routine also stimulates our creativity and larger thinking; it is not wasted time. A special place for these activities is not wasted space either.

Honoring Our Holy of Holies

Sometimes reclaiming time and space for our selves can feel indulgent, but it is all right to make it a priority. Of the three spaces in the Tabernacle, the Holy of Holies was the most protected and honored, which in turn invites us to take the same care and attention with our own personal spaces. Putting a few boundaries into place is an effective way to begin honoring our Holy of Holies. George, a participant in one of my sacred space retreats, recalls creating his personal space. While shopping with his wife at a local furniture store, he spotted a colorful chair and remarked, "That's perfect." His wife looked puzzled by his comment because they weren't looking for chairs. He explained it was going to be his sacred space chair and that he planned to place it near the window where the afternoon sunlight floods through the panes of glass in their living room. Wanting to carve out a quiet space for himself, he asked his wife to honor his intention to cultivate an open heart and quiet mind. Whenever she sees him in the chair she knows not to interrupt him or seek out conversation.

at home where he liked to read and prepare sermons, his wife and children would invariably wander in looking for lost toys or a mislaid stapler, or to just to be with him. Sometimes he welcomed their presence, but other times it felt like an intrusion into his time alone. To reclaim some quiet space, he discussed his need for privacy with his wife. Together they came up with a solution. Now a small needlepoint sign hangs off the doorknob to Danny's office. One side of the sign reads *welcome* and the other side reads *do not disturb*. This gives Danny the time and space he needs to relax into solitude but also and lets his family know when he's open to visitors.

Paula told me her story of vacationing with extended family at a beach house on Cape Cod. Four sisters and their husbands and a total of 12 children gather annually for a week by the ocean. With all the commotion of people coming and going and keeping track of sunscreen, boogie boards, sandals, and towels, the sisters felt

Between an active family life and the demands of his congregation, Danny, the father of two small children and the associate minister at a local church, had little time for himself. Though he had an office distracted from their primary purpose for the trip—girl time. They soon came up with a creative idea to remedy their problem. After setting up their chairs, towels, and umbrellas on the beach, they drew a large circle in the sand that encompassed the four chairs. For two hours each day, children and husbands were not allowed to cross over the line so the sisters could enjoy reconnecting with one another inside their protective circle.

A playful boundary kept this sacred space safe from interruptions.

In each of these stories, George, Danny, and Paula asked for what they wanted and their families were more than willing to accommodate them. Taking the time and space they needed for themselves overflowed to their families. By being attentive to their own needs they were able to be more attentive to their loved ones. By listening to their own hearts, they were able to listen to others. Each person expressed an increased appreciation for his or her family after spending time alone or with sisters in Paula's case. As we look at the rooms and spaces in our homes, we can brainstorm ideas for creating a space for ourselves if one doesn't exist. If we already have a place, maybe it needs some attention or we realize we've abandoned it. Perhaps it's time to dust it off and use it again?

There should be at least a room, or some corner where no one will find you and disturb you or notice you. You should be able to untether yourself from the world and set yourself free, loosing all the fine strings and strands of tension that bind you . . .

~ Thomas Merton
Catholic monk, poet, & author

A Space of One's Own

Virginia Woolf describes the significance of having a private space in her book A Room of One's Own. It was written at a time when female authors were relegated to the parlor in the company of family and friends while writing because private space was inaccessible to them. Though she advocated specifically for women, Woolf's message holds true for all people. We need a place of our own, a Holy of Holies. Joan Anderson describes her private space in her book, A Year by the Sea: "I've created a room of my own off the kitchen, with windows facing the woods, my only statement (to myself actually) that I must remain my own person. I've had the notion ever since a therapist friend showed me her sparsely furnished tower room with a view of the Hudson River. 'I permit only objects and people of my choosing here,' she said. 'I want pure space with no negative energy, just for myself.'"

These kinds of individual spaces are a counterbalance to the public areas of a home and are seldom given the attention they deserve. As an architect, I have noticed that common rooms such as kitchens, master suites, and great rooms are the primary focus in home design with little energy given to personal and private spaces, areas for quiet reflection and creative endeavors. Our American culture encourages a fast-paced life – to be still or non-productive can almost feel like death, and our homes are often a reflection of this value. However, once we start allowing Sabbath time, a place to slow down a bit, we find our life expands. We don't need huge chunks of time, and the spaces we make do not necessarily need to be a separate room. An alcove in a hallway with a soft chair, a desk niche in the corner of a room, or a workbench in the garage devoted to tying flies is sufficient. It may also be a specific time of day when a room is quiet and empty, a time when we can enjoy a moment of solitude.

Valerie describes her Holy of Holies this way, "Lately there is a chair in the corner of my office that feels sacred to me. I find myself landing there to pray, journal, and read sacred texts. On the wall on one side of the chair is a collage I made 13 years ago, intentionally envisioning my future. On the wall on the other side is a small piece of art that includes these words: There is nothing more powerful than a woman with an open heart. The room itself is my space, where I work and write, but the chair and the corner feel sacred to me."

Matt, a father of four, found personal space by rising early each morning before heading into his office in downtown St. Louis. His morning routine includes retrieving the newspaper from the front yard and brewing a pot of coffee in the kitchen. When he opens the front door to his two-story brick home with black wooden shutters flanking the windows, the

Quiet places in a home counter balance the active areas of a dwelling creating a harmonious environment.

first thing he sees is the deep blue shade of the sky that ushers in the coming dawn. Small droplets of water cling to the blades of grass, and he feels the cool moisture on his bare feet as he walks across the lawn. Inside, the kitchen stands empty and still, awaiting the morning light. Sitting at the antique table that belonged to his grandmother, he holds a warm mug of coffee in his hands, anticipating the rich flavor of his brew as he takes his first sip. Upstairs, his family sleeps soundly in their beds. He peruses the paper, pausing at the sports section where he reads statistics about favorite players and local teams. It is the one time of day that is his own, a time to hear his own thoughts uninterrupted by conversations or requests.

Similarly, Larry, a pharmacist from a local drug store in the Midwest, has an evening ritual to decompress after a long day of standing at a counter filling prescriptions. Each night after returning from work, he kicks off his shoes and sinks into his velour reclining chair in the wood-paneled den near the kitchen. A bookcase lines the walls and large beams span the ceiling above. With all the lights turned off and only a glow emanating from the fish tank, his den is transformed into a personal retreat. He lingers for long periods of time watching the fluid motion of the exotic tropical fish as they duck and dart through faux coral. He savors their vivid colors and stripes in fluorescent orange, indigo blue, yellow, black, and iridescent white. The stress of the day washes away as he takes in the intricate details of each fish swimming effortlessly in the water. These evening "sitting sessions" have become an essential part of his day, and he is content while in the safe haven of his den.

Along with finding a place and time of day to just be in our homes, creating a physical space solely for our selves is a valuable experience. A room of our own seems to say, "Yes, you are important enough to make space for." It is here that we can quiet our minds and tap into the inner wisdom that nurtures and sustains us. Adam rediscovered his love of woodworking when he created a workshop for himself above the garage of his log cabin. As a teenager, he spent hours in his high school shop class designing and producing fine pieces of furniture. Running his hands across the grain of pine, oak, or mahogany boards, he feels the texture of the wood, and his love of building furniture is renewed. The smell of wood in the air, the sound of the table saw as it slices through a board, the feel of a chisel in his hands or the fine dust that settles on the floor as he's working bring a deep sense of satisfaction. He feels at home in his woodshop, a place that is sacred to him. As he immerses himself in the details of a project, a solution will often present itself to some challenge he's been facing. It's as if occupying his hands and mind opens up other creative channels within himself.

Tammy, a young mother of two preschool boys, longed for a space of her own uncluttered with Legos, toy trucks, and the noise of rambunctious play, a place where she could read, pay bills, and dabble in her hobby of writing poetry. In the corner of her kitchen, a small counter area with phone books stacked to one side and unpaid bills piled on the other was the only space she claimed for herself. Above the counter, coupons, schedules, photographs of her family, and crayon drawings by her children were randomly tacked to a bulletin board hanging on the wall. Whenever she tried to sit down to work at her kitchen desk, she was constantly interrupted. Tammy began to dream about creating a space for herself that was separate from the ebb and flow of family life. She decided to convert a large storage closet into a small office. By adding a built-in desk along the length of the wall with a hanging bookcase above it and a window to frame a view of a large pine tree outside, the storage closet was transformed into a modest retreat space. The minute Tammy enters the room, she feels calm and clear-minded, happy for time alone.

Another young mother expressed a similar desire. "With two small children in my home, I find it really difficult to preserve an area that doesn't get cluttered with kids' toys, cups, drawing, and loose socks. Sacred to me would be an area that is clean and clear and uncluttered, where every item in sight doesn't remind me of something I have to do—but instead, a place where I can just be." Our personal space may be created for more traditional forms of meditation and prayer too. These spaces beckon us to take time for tending the soul and to be still for a few moments. The very presence of a Holy of Holies grants permission to take time out of our day for spiritual encounters.

We may find our personal space expanding into other areas of our home—the sun-drenched kitchen nook inspires us to grab our journal and write for a few minutes; the guitar by the fireplace lures us to play a song or two. Just as our physical space seems to expand, so does our interior space. We suddenly have compassion for the old man living alone next door, we have random moments of gratitude, or we laugh more. Having a Holy of Holies that honors our interior journey can be a transforming experience. It provides a calm place that balances the more active areas of our dwelling. It's where we touch base with our soul—the part of us that is timeless, generous, and full of grace.

A Retreat for Couples

The couple's realm needs to be the kind of place that one might sit in and talk privately, perhaps with its own entrance to the outdoors . . . a world in which the intimacy of the man and woman, their joys and sorrows, can be shared and lived through.

~ Christopher Alexander
Author, architect, & professor

Having a Holy of Holies to share as a couple has a profound impact on the relationship. It offers a place to reconnect with our partner, putting aside the other roles and responsibilities that demand our focus and energy. Time spent together in a sacred space can solidify bonds of love and mutual respect and help us weather the transitions, conflicts, or challenges we face. My husband and I have a sitting room off our bedroom where we enjoy a cup of hot tea together each morning. Two soft chairs with cotton throw blankets angle towards each other with an ottoman in between. The windows in the room face west and frame a view of the Flatiron Mountains. An oriental rug, a bookcase filled with books, coffee mugs, and photographs, along with a small table for a teapot complete the space. This has been the place where we discuss a variety of topics from household repairs and schedules to the dreams we had the night before. We say a quick prayer and hug good-bye before heading off in separate directions.

Lately our morning ritual has begun to shift and seems to mirror the new phase of life we are entering as a couple. With the departure of our youngest son to college, we are now empty nesters. Our shared morning tea has been replaced by a protein fruit smoothie that makes the kitchen nook a more convenient place to be. We sometimes meet in our sitting room and other times at the kitchen table but haven't settled into a new routine as yet. A large flat-screened TV has been added to the sitting room behind my chair, a compromise that took some negotiation that's symbolic of the give-and-take of marriage. It seems fitting as we transition into this new season of life that our sacred space may need adjusting as well. We have discussed replacing the wooden kitchen table in the nook with two soft chairs, a small side table, and a place for a coffee pot and blender. I am excited about the possibilities for our new space, both the physical space in the nook and the space opened up for my husband and me to explore.

Kathy, a woman who participated in my Sacred Space workshop, described the Holy of Holies she and her partner created in their home. Two chairs were added to a sun room filled with overflowing plants and daylight streaming through floor-to-ceiling windows. Every afternoon they meet in their space to unwind and catch up with the events from each other's day. Pausing in the evenings to acknowledge one another's presence has deepened their appreciation, understanding, and love for one another. Kathy has also noticed that if they've had a conflict or need to discuss a difficult issue, they are both drawn to their sacred space because it is seasoned with positive encounters and feels like a safe place to talk.

In contrast, Pete and Sarah stumbled onto their sacred space by accident. As an event planner for a national organization, Pete is required to travel extensively for several months a year. During this time an old back injury tends to flare up due to the added stress. His wife suggested they install a hot tub on their back deck to help alleviate his back pain. As a master gardener, Sarah fills her backyard with lavish plants and flowers and vines that weave through an arched trellis. It's a luxurious spot for soaking in warm water and being

*Outdoor areas can be a wonderful place for a
couple's Holy of Holies*

soothed by pulsating jets. It wasn't long before Sarah began to join Pete in the hot tub, bringing along two glasses of refreshing iced tea. Soon it became a daily ritual whenever Pete was in town. Though the original intent for the hot tub was to relieve Pete's muscle tension, it became the place where Sarah and Pete catch up with one another during his season of traveling. Undisturbed by children, phones, and other distractions, they can listen to one another with focused attention.

A couple's retreat space may shift over time, but there are numerous possibilities for creating a place to be together. Adding this type of retreat space may involve some sleuthing. When do we tend to check in with one another? What do we enjoy doing together? What changes would we need to make to allow time and space to be together? Two musicians made a niche near their family room for a piano, guitars, violins, and drums. Here they rekindle their passion for music and their enjoyment of experiencing it together.

Regardless of the activity, having a place set aside to share with a partner deepens the relationship.

A Child's Hide-Away

A space of one's own is just as important for children as it is for adults. Children seem to have a natural understanding of their need for alone places and find imaginative ways to create spaces for themselves. I became particularly aware of this phenomenon on my family's annual camping trip to Moab, Utah. After setting up tents, putting lawn chairs around a fire ring, and hanging the solar shower, my children would dash off with their friends in search of a secret hideout amidst the orange sandstone cliffs and crevices. Stacking rocks and piling driftwood, they'd create a children's space tucked into a cranny behind a large group of boulders separated from the adults. Whenever we went camping, the pattern of seeking out a secret place to play repeated itself again and again.

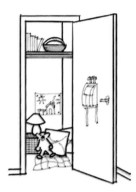

A closet nook works well for a child's special place.

Having a special place in our homes specifically for children nurtures this intuitive and creative part of a child's being and cultivates curiosity. It also provides a safe spot for a child to be when feeling insecure. A corner in my children's closets be-

came that special place of their own when they were still in preschool. Both my son and daughter were excited about making a private nook for themselves. We began the process with a visit to the local paint store to select colors for the walls, a deep pink for my daughter and midnight blue for my son. Our next trip was to Target where we purchased large pillows to place on the floor and glow-in-the-dark stars to stick on the ceiling. We emptied their closets, painted the walls a fresh new color, and neatly placed their clothes to one side of the hanging rod. The other side of the closet became the perfect child-sized niche. Katie and Will gathered their favorite books, stuffed toys, and quilts to add to their cubbyhole. Low on the wall we hung pictures they had drawn and plugged in a small lamp for reading.

They made up their own rules for their spaces too. Unless invited, no one was allowed into his or her closet, and they could choose to decorate it however they liked. Snuggled in their blankets, they'd thumb through picture books or listen to stories using their plastic tape recorder with bright red, blue, and yellow buttons. If they were upset, they often retreated to the safety of their closet space to calm themselves. As they moved through elementary school, ribbons from horse shows, trophies from soccer teams, and photographs of classmates replaced the crayon drawings and stuffed toys, but the heart of their spaces remained the same.

Connie describes the special place she created for her three children on the weekends. Every Friday evening before going to bed she packed a breakfast picnic for each of her children. Using three bandanas, she placed a mini box of cereal, a small carton of milk, a plastic spoon and bowl, an orange wedge, and a yogurt in the square pieces of cloth, and then carefully tied the corners together. On the kitchen table, she left three new books she had checked out from the local library. Attached to the books was a yellow sticky note boldly displaying the name of

each child. In the morning, her children would traipse into the kitchen to retrieve their satchel from the refrigerator, pick up a book, and head back to their room for a private picnic on their bed. This was the only time her children were allowed to take food into their bedrooms. Sometimes Connie included a small puzzle or game in the sack as a surprise. Her motivation was a few extra hours of sleep on Saturday mornings, but the picnic breakfast in bed became a time and place her children looked forward to every weekend.

Though children will find nooks and crannies for themselves, providing a formal place supports their natural tendency toward creating personal space. These do not need to be large areas or even permanent. It could be a corner in a room with a small chair and a few toys and books, a yoga mat or rug that defines the edges of a space and can be rolled up and moved to different areas of the home, a tree house or pup tent in the back yard, or even the space under a dining table with a long tablecloth enclosing it. The 1950's children's book, A Little House of Your Own, by Beatrice Schenk De Regniers, sums up the need for a Holy of Holies well: "Everyone has to have a little house of his own. Every boy has to have his own little house. Every girl should have a little house to herself. And one more thing is important too . . . When you are in your own little house no one should bother you. Everyone should leave you alone if you want to be alone."

Children are naturals at finding secret hide-outs and sacred places for themselves.

Exercises

1. If time, money, and resources were not an obstacle, what would your Holy of Holies be? This is a time to dream. Using a sketch notebook and crayons, colored pencils, or images cut from magazines; begin to envision your space. What would you be doing? What objects would you include? What are the physical characteristics of the space? How would you feel there?

2. At the top of a sheet of paper make three columns and label them Individual, Couple, and Child. Describe the characteristics of each of these private spaces in your home. If you don't have a Holy of Holies, dream up ideas for creating one.

3. Where do you naturally tend to relax with your partner in your home? Experiment with different locations in your home, perhaps sitting on the back deck in the evening, sharing a cup of coffee at the

kitchen table in the morning, or lingering over a meal in the dining room. Note
if there is a particular place that you
both like being. Are there simple adjustments that could transform it into a retreat
space? What would you include in your
ideal couple's space? Privacy is important,
but other elements may be necessary too.
Perhaps your space would need a door
that can be shut, soft chairs or a couch,
a small table, a lot of windows, earthy or
bright colors, plants, pillows, candles,
water, musical instruments, stereo, photographs, or artwork. Begin collecting
images of spaces that capture the essence
of what you'd like your space to be like
and add them to your sketchbook.

4. Brainstorm ideas with your children for
their personal space. Where will it be
located? How will it be decorated? What
items will be included? Will it be indoors
or outdoors, permanent or portable? In
your journal, make a list of items you need
to purchase, such as paint, fabric, art supplies, or a rug.

Notes

Rules of Thumb

• Everyone in your household needs a space to call their own. Consider carving out individual space within the context of a larger room.

• Don't forget the kids. Creating a special place for children can be playful and fun. They can be temporary, permanent, or portable. It can be a castle made from an appliance box or a bed loft with a ladder.

• Don't forget the adults. Couples often share a bedroom so extra effort may be needed to find a space for each individual.

• When deciding on a private space, keep in mind your senses, especially your sense of sound. Choose a place away from the most active areas of your home.

• Consider a portable personal space. A Sacred Space chest may hold art supplies, sewing notions, or other tools that can be brought out and used daily without requiring a separate area. Using a folding screen that can be stored away after use works well too. Take a 5-10 minute break in your day to spend time in your private place.

Chapter 4

More Patterns of Sacred Space

Your sacred space is where you find yourself again and again.

~ Joseph Campbell
American mythologist, writer, & lecturer

Doorways

The experience of entering a building influences the way you feel inside the building. If the transition is too abrupt there is no feeling of arrival, and the inside of the building fails to be an inner sanctum. .

~ Christopher Alexander
Author, architect, & professor

Beyond the pattern of three (public, private, and intimate space), the Tabernacle reveals other archetypal patterns that are important in our homes. One of those patterns is the experience of entering a space. Thresholds and doorways are the markers that guide us as we move into a room or building. Ancient sacred structures often had a series of gates or doorways that led to the inner sanctum. The Tabernacle had three veils, or curtains, that separated each space and marked the boundary between ordinary and sacred space. In Hebrew the word veil literally means to separate. Entrances provide a place for us to physically and psychologically shift from the clamor of the outside world into the refuge within our home. They act as a boundary and are the gateways to the ebb and flow of daily living, directing movements in, out, and through our homes.

Frank Lloyd Wright believed that the entrance into a building was crucial to the overall experience of the space. He often used a concept called compression and expansion in his designs as a way to mark the transition from one space to another. A person would pass through a low, narrow doorway or under a dropped ceiling feeling

The low ceiling over the entry door expands into a vaulted ceiling which heightens the experience when entering this home.

a sense of compression before entering a new area where the space expanded in all directions. The experience of arrival was powerful. At Taliesin West, his studio in Arizona, he would meet with new clients in an open outdoor courtyard reminiscent of the Tabernacle's Court. Sitting under a shade tree, they chatted and got to know one another. He would then usher them along a walkway toward his office, passing a decorative mosaic embedded in the pavers that signaled the entrance into a new area. Continuing through a low doorway, clients would duck their heads as they walked into his workspace. Here the focus of the conversation shifted from pleasantries to business. He was very conscious of the transition between spaces and used them to heighten a person's awareness of movement into a new place.

Interior doorways convey important information about the accessibility of various places within the walls of our home. A small solid door might suggest a private area while glass French doors imply

a permeable boundary. Doorways with unique characteristics increase the level of anticipation as a person moves through a home. An ornate curtain woven four inches thick separated the Holy of Holies from the other spaces within the Tabernacle and signaled that the place being entered was holy ground. Father Dave, a monk and teacher, created an entrance to his own Holy of Holies that touched into this archetypal pattern. He has an affinity for the South American saint known as The Lady of Guadalupe. In his small dwelling, his bedroom has a simple altar placed on top of a dresser where he prays and meditates. Hanging across the doorway to his bedroom is a strand of vertical beads with the image of The Lady of Guadalupe. Each time he passes through the beads, he is reminded of her presence with him.

Secret doorways, reminiscent of childhood experiences, tap into our love of mystery and make a place feel special by limiting the access to it. Along with a sense of in-

This narrow doorway off the master bedroom leads to a hidden office nestled above the garage.

trigue, hidden doors have served practical purposes throughout history as well. Kings and queens were afforded the freedom to come and go from their castle as they moved undetected in secret underground passageways that also served as escape routes when danger was imminent. Captivated by the idea of a hidden entrance, Dave and Barb added a concealed doorway to their children's playroom. Tucked into the back of a clothes closet, a small plywood panel opened into an attic area over the garage where the children's toys were stored. Crawling through the small opening into the attic engaged the children's sense of imagination and transformed the attic space into a magical play world.

The doorways in our home can enhance our experience of a space if we are attentive to this archetypal pattern. When they are open, doors welcome people into the inner sanctuary of our dwelling, but when closed, they offer privacy and protection. Both are needed. They also mark the transition between rooms and give us clues about the space we are entering, whether it is open and public or hidden and private. Like the physical doors of our dwelling, we have inner doors too, doors that lead to our heart, mind, and spirit. It is worth noticing the connection between the two. As we walk through our front door at home we might ponder the question, "What people and opportunities do I want to be open to in my life right now?" Or "What things do I need to leave behind and not allow in?" Sometimes shutting these inner doors is as gentle as closing up a summer cottage when the season has ended or as harsh as a slamming screen door against a violent storm. Openings can come in similar ways: effortlessly, like a budding flower, or boldly, like a bright light at the end of a dark alley directing us forward. Regardless of where we find them, doorways invite us to pay attention to the changing terrain around us, and whether it is a physical shift or an internal shift, we can pause at the threshold before moving forward.

Meaningful Objects

I know a cure for sadness: Let your hands touch something that makes your eyes smile. I bet there are a hundred objects close by that can do that.

~ Mira
Poet from India, 1498-1550

Along with paying attention to doorways, another lesson the Tabernacle teaches us is the significance of meaningful objects. Special objects, talismans, and relics were an integral part of many ancient sacred places, and the Tabernacle was filled with them. These holy objects connected the Jewish people to their history, to God, and to one another and were a reflection of what they held dear. Their most precious objects were placed within the Holy of Holies. Here a golden box known as the Ark of the Covenant held the Ten Commandments, a symbol of Divine guidance. Also within the box was a golden pot of manna, both physically and spiritually representing God's sustaining power among the people. Lastly, the budding rod of Aaron, the original high priest, was placed inside the Ark as a reminder to all priests to blossom and bear fruit.

In Jerusalem, the foundation of the old temple called the Wailing Wall has become a sacred object for the city. Constructed from large stones, it draws pilgrims from around the world who offer their prayers and requests to the Divine. Groups of people linger in prayer nearby as supplicants tuck small pieces of paper with the names of loved ones into the cracks between the rocks. Beverly, a hospital chaplain, had visited the wall and remembers placing her open hands just a few inches away from the stones. She recalls feeling an energy that was almost palpable and a sense that she was on holy ground. Not far away, she picked up a pebble from the road and slipped it into her pocket. Whenever she touches it, she is reminded of her experience in Jerusalem and the nearness of her Creator. The small rock has become her personal sacred object.

Similarly, a chime, an eagle's feather, a cross, a lock of hair, a photograph, or a small statuette can be a physical reminder of our beliefs, hopes, experiences, and visions. These objects ground us to our past and our memories; they connect us to our dreams and visions; and they remind us that we are not alone in the universe, that others have shared our experiences. Meaningful objects make our homes personal and thereby sacred. Incorporating this pattern is especially significant for our personal spaces. The old advice given to a bride before she weds to wear "something old, something new, something borrowed, and something blue" resonates with our desire to have objects we love near by, close to our body.

Margaret, a writer and event planner, has a small, upholstered rocking chair that belonged to her grandmother in her home office. Layers of slipcovers mark the many seasons this chair has traveled through the life of the family, and the original material is still intact though tattered with age. Margaret loves to sit in this chair because she feels enveloped by the memories of her grandmother, her childhood, and the women in her family history. It is here that she experiences the feminine qualities of God.

Another writer, Kent Haruf, has his office in what was formerly the coal room in the basement of his Southern Illinois home. His desk is cluttered with an assortment of objects and talismans he's collected over a lifetime that are meaningful to him. A skull of a Hereford

Meaningful objects, such as photographs of loved ones, antique dishes, a favorite piece of art, or religious icons form a tangible link between a person and a room.

bull hanging on a nail, brown wrapping paper tacked on the wall for taking notes, his daughter's artwork, landscape paintings, a bird's nest, black turf from Northern Ireland, a piece of bark from William Faulkner's home, and an arrowhead are a few of his objects. He describes how having these items nearby changes the space. "I do not pay much attention to these things, but having them there makes a difference. The things I have on my desk are important to me. It's an emotional attachment to all these things that connects me up with the impulse to write. Every time I go down to work, I feel as if I'm descending into a sacred place."

A friend once asked me to help her transform a room that was rarely used in her home into a place for reading, writing, and meditation. As we talked through some ideas, specific objects came to mind that were important for her to have in the space—photographs of her ancestors, a painting of the first church where she officiated as an ordained priest, a cross,

candles, and shells collected from her favorite beach, as well as several books, including her journal. These were the things that anchored her and made the room her own. By offering the familiarity of her history, the objects made her feel secure enough to explore new dreams from a safe place. Whether the meaningful objects we include in our home are modest or elaborate, they deepen our connection to the place we live. They are a tangible reminder of what is important to us. They remind us of the people we love, the places we have been, and the experiences that have been significant in our life. Amulets sometimes come in the form of a person. This is someone in our life who is a touchstone, bringing us back to our center where we can relax and be content with our self. It could be a grandparent, a dear friend, or a teacher. Like the meaningful objects in our home, they capture the qualities of God we cherish and invite us to become a grounding point for others as well.

Rituals are one way in which attention is paid. Rituals arise from the stages and ages of life. Rituals transform the ordinary into the holy.

~ Robert Fulghum
Author

Rituals

The rhythms of rituals performed by people and priests in the Tabernacle transformed the otherwise ordinary tent into a place rich with meaning. As people gathered in the court, priests prepared themselves to enter the holy place of God by washing their hands and feet, a symbolic gesture of purification. Water for the ritual was held in a large vessel known as the brazen laver outside the entrance to the tent. Inside the holy place was a golden candelabrum, a table with an offering of bread, and an altar with burning incense. Priests tended the altar daily, and as smoke rose from the hot coals it was believed the people's prayers ascended to God. Similarly, present-day monasteries and retreat centers are embedded with rituals and often have a peaceful atmosphere due to the observance of daily prayer and silence.

One such place is the hermitage of St. Francis of Assisi. Located in the northern region of Italy known as Umbria, the hermitage sits above the city along the cliffs overlooking the valley below. It is here where Saint Francis would retreat from the clamor and trappings of the city seeking silence, prayer, and closeness to God. Pilgrims still make the trek up the steep slope to this retreat where they meander quietly along paths that weave through the forest and cliffs. Makeshift altars of stone appear along the trails, and the gray face of the cliffs has turned white from the thousands of crosses etched across the surface. Even the ground is covered with small crosses fashioned from sticks and branches. The impulse to make a cross is a ritual that grew organically from those who sojourned to the top of the hill and has transformed the trees, the rocks, the sky, and the ground into a holy sanctuary.

Our rituals may not be quite as elaborate as those performed in the Tabernacle or involve climbing a steep hill toward a hermitage, but they are just as important and they matter in creating sacred space.

*Rituals mark major events in one's life but are
also embedded in the rhythm of daily living.*

We live ritualized lives, and our personal rituals have the power to affect our dwellings in a positive way. In his book From Beginning to End, the Rituals of Our Life, Robert Fulghum calls attention to the daily and seasonal rituals common to us all: eating a meal together, celebrating birthdays and anniversaries, or simply walking the dog. Like the string in a strand of pearls, rituals hold the seasons and experiences in our life together and connect us to the universal human story. They mark special occasions and transitions, provide a framework for connection with others and with God, and sustain us in times of uncertainty. Rituals bring meaning and stability to our lives.

Graduations, weddings, and funerals are rituals that mark major passages in our lives, but there are many subtle ways we calibrate our day as well. We may not be aware of our personal rituals because repeated patterns of behavior are familiar and often done with little forethought. These quieter rituals are significant be-cause they connect us with a specific place in our home. Maybe we tuck our child into bed with a lullaby, listen to the sports update on the radio in the shower before heading to work, eat breakfast in bed on birthdays, or cook pancakes in the kitchen on Saturday mornings. Whatever our rituals may be, many of them happen within the walls of our home.

Children are naturals at creating rituals. Remember the secret password or handshake needed to enter the fort or pricking a finger to draw blood to become a member of the club or clicking a flashlight on and off to signal a special code? These childhood rituals changed an ordinary day into a day full of mystery. They instilled a sense of vibrancy for life, something Pat, a middle-aged woman, felt she had lost. She noticed her relationship with her husband had settled into a complacent routine, and she felt stuck in a rut. She wanted to recapture some of the delight they knew when they first met.

Both Pat and her husband worked full-time, but she usually returned home from work thirty minutes before he did. She would hear the garage door open at exactly the same time every evening, signaling her husband's return. This seemed to be the perfect occasion to try something new. She chose a simple ritual of lighting a candle near the door where her husband entered every afternoon. About ten minutes before he came home, she faithfully lit the candle. Even if she was in the office or walking the dog when he arrived, he saw the large Mexican candle flickering on a rustic wood table and knew she was thinking of him. The entry vestibule became a sacred portal welcoming him home. If they had a disagreement, it became a symbol of her willingness to reconcile. The observance of this daily ritual over several years made returning home after a long day feel like a welcoming embrace to both of them and brought new life to their relationship.

Having a ritual and a place where we can reconnect with our core or with significant people in our life opens the door to grace-filled moments. A neighbor describes an encounter with God while sitting on her back patio early one morning. It was her habit to spend a little time outside each morning in the spring and summer when the weather had changed enough that the air was crisp but not cold. It was a quiet time of the day before cars rumbled past her home or dogs began to bark, announcing their presence. She enjoyed the few minutes of stillness before heading off for a three-mile run. Snuggled in a blanket with a hot cup of tea, she would watch clouds change from gray to pink as the sun rose.

On one particular morning she was overcome with a feeling of being timeless and magically connected to the best part of herself, the part that felt untainted by her limitations, shortcomings, circumstances, or history. She became deeply aware of the Divine presence being so close that there seemed to be no separation. She felt at one with her surroundings, the grass, the trees, the morning light, and the wildlife rustling the nearby bushes. The brief encounter lingered with her throughout the day. She was grateful for her garden patio and her morning ritual that created an opening for her enchanted morning experience.

Rituals cause us to pause for a moment and become realigned with a purpose beyond day-to-day tasks. Yes, we need to go to work, buy groceries, pay bills, or repair the fence, but we also need to be aware of the larger context in which these activities are done. We may cook a family dinner to satisfy hungry appetites, but our underlying longing may be to nurture and sustain family bonds of love. Blowing out candles on a birthday cake reminds us that each day is a gift, and hanging sheets on a line to dry connects us with a memory of handing clothespins to our grandmother. Our rituals, large or small, happen in a physical context, perhaps at a kitchen counter, a dining room table, the bathroom shower, or our prayer corner. Like the desert sanctuary of the Israelites, our home is the container that holds our rituals, grounding them in a specific time and place.

Prayer

Prayer sets no goals - other than deep, open availability to God's presence.

~ Cynthia Bourgeault
Author, teacher, & priest

It's hard to imagine a sacred space without prayer. Whatever form it takes, prayer is a universal experience in sanctuaries throughout the world, including the Tabernacle where an altar of incense burned day

and night, symbolic of prayers continuously rising toward heaven. Monasteries have a rhythm of prayer beginning in the dark hours of the morning, and the call to prayer echoes across Muslim nations in the middle of the day. As the day draws to a close, chanting of vespers can often be heard drifting through the doors of a chapel. We have our own patterns of prayer too—a quiet moment in the morning to read words of inspiration, holding hands to offer a blessing before eating a meal, or stilling our hearts as we reflect on the day's events. Prayer opens our heart to God's presence in the midst of life. It can take many forms, but underneath is a desire to be aligned with goodness and truth. There are prayers of blessing, prayers of asking for help, silent prayers of contemplation, prayers of listening, prayers of action, prayers of movement, prayers of gratitude, prayers of healing, prayers of welcome, and prayers for others. Just as our rituals happen in the context of a physical space, so do our prayers, and the

different rooms in our home can evoke different types of prayer. The Holy of Holies in our home is where we rekindle our love for self and God, but the other rooms in our home invite prayers of a different kind.

Every room in our home evokes a prayer. Bedrooms invite prayers for rest and intimacy, family rooms invite prayers of gathering and community, recreation rooms invite prayers for play and renewal, and gardens invite prayers for grounding and connection with the earth. As we move through our home we can pause in each space and listen to whatever hopes, dreams, and prayers are stirred in our heart by being in this place. The kitchen is where we cook and create meals, so prayers about sustenance may be brought to mind by the space. We might ask for our daily bread, both food for our body and food for our soul, remembering we are held and sustained by a loving power. Maybe we need patience or courage to confront a colleague or stamina to get through another day of work. As we eat our oatmeal we might imagine God's grace filling us and sticking to our ribs like a hearty meal. Thich Nhat Hanh, a Buddhist monk, offers prayers of gratitude when he eats his food, taking in the color, the flavor, and the texture of each bite and imagining the person who tended the field as well as the rain and the sun that made his meal possible.

Bathrooms bring to mind both release and cleansing. A dear spiritual companion describes soaking in her bathtub. When the tub is full, she feels a weightlessness and lightness to her body that lifts her spirit and relaxes her muscles. She chooses to linger in the tub as the water swirls down the drain, offering a prayer of letting go. As the water continues to disappear and the weight returns to her body, she imagines her irritation with the car mechanic, her anxiety about finances, and her stubborn back pain being washed away with the water. In such a way our home becomes a place that continually reminds us of God's presence, wherever we are or whatever we may be doing. The rooms, nooks, corners, and closets in our home beckon us to hear their songs of love, nurture, and support. When Janet was repairing a deck over her garage that was weather beaten by the harsh mountain sun, she began to feel into the energy that was part of this outdoor space. Lingering on the deck she was inspired to write down prayers on slips of paper and stuff them between the two by fours of the new privacy wall being built around the perimeter of the deck. Her prayers included words like peace, warmth, sunshine, light, nature, and serenity. She added favorite poems about the outdoors by Mary Oliver and Ralph Waldo Emerson, and she included words of praise by Rumi and Hafiz. In a similar gesture, my great-grandfather, who was a Polish immigrant and a stone mason, would write poetry in his native tongue and put the crumpled pieces of paper into the hollow cavity of the cinder block walls he was constructing. I'm not sure these were prayers, but I like to think so. Sometimes our home has an overall prayer that holds all the other prayers together. This was my experience at our cabin in Fraser, Colorado.

Before my husband and I began construction on our cabin, we spent many nights on the densely forested land, either in a pup tent or in our camper. Our property is on a south sloping hill that overlooks a valley with a small stream running through it surrounded by clumps of reeds and grasses. On our first camp out with our children, we happened upon a porcupine as we neared our site. We've seen a newborn moose with her mother, two male bull moose sparring, beavers slapping their tails on the water as the sound reverberated up the valley, foxes diving in the snow as they hunted their prey, coyotes roaming the hills, and meteor showers in the night sky. A stray buffalo even meandered by one afternoon. Up the road is a youth camp where teenagers come to enjoy the outdoors and hear about God. The land

has a spiritual and peaceful feeling to it, and before we began building our cabin we felt compelled to pray that the essence of the land be captured in its walls. We had some other ideas of our own too, but the overwhelming sense was that it be a place for retreat and renewal. Many family gatherings, reunions, weddings, engagements, and retreats have seasoned the cabin with laughter, tears, and joy. The prayers embodied in the land and the cabin have been a blessing to those who have come.

Listening Prayer

The following exercise will help articulate your dreams, intentions, and prayers for a specific room in your home. It begins by focusing attention on your body to become present to your physicality then shifts awareness to the space surrounding you. Choose a room where you want to listen to the prayers that are evoked by the space.

Meditation Exercise

Stand with your arms comfortably resting at your sides and your legs hip-width apart. Bring attention to your breath and breathe deeply. Tilt your head to one side and gently pull with your hand for a deeper stretch. Repeat this on the other side. Now tilt your head forward and roll down slowly, bending your knees slightly and letting your head and arms hang loose. Roll up and stretch to the sky. Release your arms and let them float down to your sides. Gently swing your arms left to right; feel your feet planted on the floor. Now you are grounded in the room. With your palms facing up in a gesture of receptivity, listen to what stirs within your heart. What are your dreams for this room? Whom do you envision here? What will you be doing? Invite God's spirit to inspire you as you listen for the prayers that bubble up. Now, raise your arms to offer your prayers into the room and to God. When you are ready, lower your arms and bring your hands to your heart as a symbol of holding your prayer within. Bring your attention back to your breath again. If you like, write down your prayers for this room.

Beauty

Never lose an opportunity of seeing anything beautiful, for beauty is God's handwriting.

~ Ralph Waldo Emerson
Author, teacher, & priest

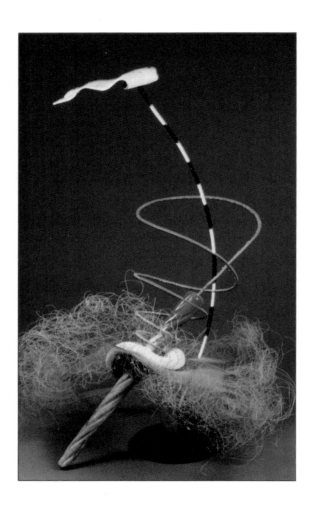

Perhaps one of the most unifying patterns found in the Tabernacle is its visual delight. Only the most skilled craftsmen were allowed to work on the tent, using precious materials for its structure and contents, such as silver, bronze, gold, linen, onyx stones, gems, and acacia wood. Every detail was meticulously spelled out, including the garments for the priests. Quality workmanship was paramount. The tent curtains were made from fine twisted linen in rich colors of blue, scarlet, and purple, and the clasps that held them together were pure gold. Beautiful objects and materials were not an afterthought but an essential element to this desert sanctuary. The lush interior seemed to stand in stark contrast to the harsh and barren landscape surrounding it, a reminder of God's presence and generous provision. Similar to rituals and prayer, beauty has a way of pulling us out of the mundane into a place of wonder and delight, which is where Spirit dwells.

Katherine recalls a trip to Vancouver Island where she visited Butchart Gardens near the port city of Victoria, British Columbia. Entering the grounds she hiked along a trail that led to the rim of what was formerly a limestone quarry. Turning the last corner as she ascended the hill, she came to an overlook with a view of a magnificent sunken garden below. It took her breath away. Vibrant purple irises, yellow daffodils, pansies, multi-colored tulips, flowering plum and cherry trees, heather and forsythia presented an abundant floral display amid the backdrop of deep green conifer trees, fountains, and ponds. Instead of a scar on the landscape, the rock crevasse in the hillside had been transformed into a wonderland of vegetation where people from around the world come to be refreshed by its splendor. Many of us have memories or experiences in our life that resemble the hollowed-out and marred earth of the rock quarry, but Butchart Gardens and places like it offer us an assurance that even our darkest moments can

yield something good. That's what beauty does. It changes the ordinary or painful into something amazing that nourishes our soul.

This sense of wonder and amazement is important in sacred spaces because it captures the essence of the Divine Mystery. Like meaningful objects, beauty reminds us of the larger context we inhabit, offering a fuller perspective that nudges us back to our center where we feel safe, secure, and loved. These are the qualities we want to have in our home as well. Visually pleasing places help us feel at ease and resonate with our desire for order. Neuro-aesthetics, a new field of study, indicates that visually pleasing environments, works of art, and music change our physiology and attitude, increase a sense of relaxation, creativity, and inspiration. The brain wave patterns produced by beauty are similar to the ones found when we pray. Beauty changes our perception of the world. How beauty is articulated in our home will vary depending on our sense of aesthetics. Some prefer sparse settings like a desert while others prefer ornate environments similar to Butchart Gardens. Both reflect different aspects of the spiritual journey and each is beautiful in its own way. Architect Ludwig Mies van der Rohe's familiar quote, "Less is more," speaks to the power of simplicity.

Taking this sentiment to heart, Vern, an architect who lived in Africa for a year, designed his home with minimal adornment. Bamboo floors contrasted with clean white walls, and horizontal metal handrails flanked the stairway. He believed the natural beauty of each material or object was highlighted when it didn't have to compete with extraneous decorations. Only one piece of art was displayed on each wall in his home, and a Persian rug was the focal point for the main living space. His experience in Africa had taught him to appreciate living an uncomplicated life, and he wanted his environment to reflect this value. To him, beauty was found in the clarity of clean lines and the spaciousness created by paring down his possessions. Sometimes we need places like Vern's to hear the still small voice within that guides us, places that are expansive and without clutter.

In contrast, Robert, a history buff, has accumulated an impressive collection of Native American relics, first edition books, antique glass, and vinyl records. His Victorian home resembles a museum where his collections are artfully displayed in rooms with weathered hardwood floors, wide oak trim, and walls accented with richly colored paint. Each room has a theme and is filled with historic memorabilia. He finds beauty in the details of a beaded Pueblo moccasin or the deep hue of the cobalt blue bottle in the windowsill. Wherever he turns in his home he can find a hand-crafted treasure that inspires him. The plethora of beautiful objects in his home is a reminder of God's abundance, and sometimes that's exactly what we need to feel connected to a Holy presence.

Regardless of how we find it, beauty speaks the language of the soul and breaks through the limitations of our thoughts, our schedules, or our particular circumstance in life. It sometimes takes us by surprise, stirring our sense of won-der, but it always invites us to pause and just enjoy what is good in the moment. We need beauty nearby, especially in our homes, as a reminder to enter this soul dialogue. Sometimes it may feel like a luxury to purchase a piece of art, but it's a necessity of the heart just as having a furnace is necessary to keep our home warm during the chill of winter. A paint-ing on the wall with vivid colors, a vase of flowers from the garden, or Mozart's music

being played on the piano pulls us into the present moment where we can savor what is beautiful and remember the goodness surrounding us.

The soft curves of this pool chair give it an elegant flair, combining function and beauty.

Exercises

1. Begin paying attention to the doorways and thresholds you encounter throughout your day. Which ones are inviting and helpful in transitioning into a new space? Which feel uncomfortable? Can you pick out the details that make an entry appealing to you? You may want to collect images of doorways and entrances from magazines, catalogues, or newspapers that portray qualities you like.

2. What are the rituals you experience in your home? Consider holidays and major family events as well as weekly or daily rituals. List your rituals according to the pattern of the Tabernacle and where they happen in your home:

   -Public rituals shared in a large context

   -Private rituals shared with 4-8 people

   -Intimate rituals done alone or shared with one other person

   Is there a balance between public, private, and intimate rituals? If not, what would you change?

3. Write about an encounter you've had with beauty and how it made you feel. Describe the details as clearly as possible. Are there places in your home that capture that feeling? Do a quick inventory of each room in your home and notice if there are any objects of beauty. If not, consider adding a splash of beauty to your home with a vase of flowers, a new piece of artwork, a colorful area rug, or even new dish towels. This doesn't need to be elaborate, just something that captures your attention.

Notes

Rules of Thumb

• Use entrances into spaces to prepare a person for a new activity. Dangle beads in the doorway into a teenager's room or try hanging wispy curtains from a cable wire to separate a sitting area from the master bedroom.

• Use outdoor rooms such as patios, covered porches, balconies, and decks as transition spaces between the interior of your home and the outdoors. If you space is limited, try placing a bistro chair with potted plants and a small fountain near an entry to create a mini outdoor area.

• All rooms in your home should have at least one sacred object. Rotating them occasionally, perhaps with the change of each season, will keep you from becoming desensitized to them.

• Notice the connection between the prayers you have for the rooms of your home and the prayers you have for the different areas of your life.

• Beauty adds inspiration to your dwelling. Surround yourself with beautiful objects. A vase of wildflowers, a bright colored coffee mug, a painting or sculpture, or the soft texture of a hand-woven throw imbue a sense of delight and abundance.

Chapter 5

Architectural Basics

Nature needs from man not imitation but interpretation.

~ Frank Lloyd Wright
Architect

Along with using the Tabernacle as a template for creating sacred environments, understanding a few principles of architecture is helpful in making a space feel inviting. One of my favorite architects was Frank Lloyd Wright, a prominent designer at the turn of the century. He was a master observer of nature, and to him most of the important principles of architecture and design could be discovered in nature. He believed the design of buildings should inspire us with beauty as well as meet practical needs. Like the seamless blend of beauty and function found in nature, he noticed how color, shape, form, and texture came together in infinite combinations to satisfy one's yearning for visual delight while offering creative solutions to functional needs. The spider's web, the coral reef, a deep river canyon, or a simple bird's nest display principles of scale, proportion, shape, and form that are guidelines for designing balanced living spaces.

These components of space—scale, proportion, shape, and form—help differentiate the public, private, and intimate places in a home and are used in sacred structures to enhance a person's experience there. The circular shape of the kiva with soft dirt floors, the rectilinear tea room with woven floor mats, the golden dome of a Buddhist shrine, the tall arched ceilings of a cathedral, or the massive scale of the pyramids are structures that blend architectural elements in extraordinary designs. Proportion, scale, shape, and form are the building blocks for creating spaces that resonate with our physical and spiritual longings.

Scale and Proportion

The soul and body are subject to the same laws of proportion that govern music and the cosmos itself. We are happiest when we conform to these laws because we love similarity.

~ Boethius
Roman philosopher & mathematician, 480-574

We intuitively sense when a place has good proportion and human scale. Our comfort level in a space is directly related to its scale and proportion. Proportion is the three-dimensional relationship between the length, width, and height of a room while scale is the relationship between the human body and the details in the room. For example, a typical door is about seven feet tall, similar to the height of a person with a raised arm over his head.

If our body is either overpowered by a space or cramped by a space, we feel uncomfortable. Though there are no fixed rules about scale and proportion, throughout history many attempts have been made to create ideal guidelines. The ancient Greeks used the golden rectangle to determine the size of a space based on a mathematical equation with a proportion of 1 to 1.6. The Japanese used a system based on the tatami, a sleeping mat that related to the human body. Palladio, an influential Italian architect from the sixteenth century, suggested the ideal proportion for a room should be as follows: the width must be at least half the length of the space and the height no less than the width of the room. Interestingly enough, the Holy Place within the Tabernacle conformed to these guidelines: it was 30 feet long, 15 feet wide, and 15 feet high. The Holy of Holies was a perfect cube, and the open-aired Court was 150 feet long by 75 feet wide, following Palladio's width and length proportional rule.

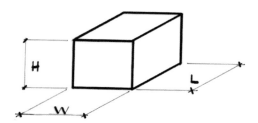

In general, a room that is shaped like an oblong cube will feel better than one that is long and skinny or tall and narrow. Think of a pear versus a celery stalk. While these guidelines are useful, it is the height of a room that significantly affects our sense of intimacy and comfort in a space. Large gatherings of people will naturally gravitate toward rooms with taller ceilings, while a low ceiling over a window seat invites quiet conversation. Changing ceiling heights throughout a home allows for varying levels of intimacy, an essential quality of sacred space.

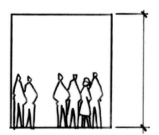 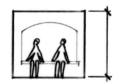

Carol and Jim found this tool helpful in the design of their home. They wanted a home with an open floor plan and vaulted ceilings to take advantage of mountain views but were concerned that they would feel dwarfed by the large volume of space. By lowering the ceiling along the perimeter of their kitchen, dining room, family room, and bedrooms, they created spaces that felt comfortable while maintaining the open feeling they desired.

Along with proportion, the scale of a room is an important factor to our sense of comfort. It provides a "human-sized" point of reference within the larger context of a space. Details that relate to the dimensions of the human body ground us in a room. The outline of an individual brick within a large brick wall relates to the size of our hand and thus connects us to the entire wall. A hearthstone in front of a fireplace relates to our hips, planks in a wood floor approximate the width of a foot, and French doors are typically the width of outstretched arms. When doors, windows, ceiling heights, and materials relate to our height, or the size of our hands, feet, arms, and legs, we feel at ease.

Scale can also be used to foster a sense of grandeur when details of the building or space are massive compared to the size of our body. It can cause us to feel awed or over-powered by the structure, and that may be the desired affect when trying to capture the essence of God. In comparison, spaces that approximate the dimensions of the human body will feel secure. In the photographs of the churches, notice the size of the doors, windows, and other details in each building. The contrast between the two shows the impact scale has on our experience of space. In our homes, the more the scale relates to the size of our body, the better it feels.

The scale of these two churches affects a person's experience in the building. Each conveys a unique perspective about sacred space.

Lee and Judy have an oversized master bedroom with a vaulted ceiling and a large picture window framing a view outside. The tall ceilings create a sense of spaciousness, but Judy, a petite woman, felt lost in the expansive volume of space. As a result she never felt completely comfortable in her bedroom, especially when she was alone at night. To bring the bedroom back into human scale, the visual height of the ceiling needed to be lowered. Judy accomplished this by adding a band of trim around the room at the same height as the door. Below the trim, walls were painted a soft purple that matched the rock outcropping in the distant hillside. The walls above the trim were painted the same cream color as the ceiling, giving the illusion of a lower ceiling and an overall experience of a smaller room. Judy says she now feels like she's nestled in a cottage instead of swimming in excessive space.

The scale of furniture and objects in a room are important too. I have a vivid memory of meeting with a young doctor in her office for a consultation. She sat behind an oversized, solid-oak desk that called attention to her petite frame. The contrast between the massive desk and her delicate features gave the impression that the desk was overwhelming her. I noticed I felt less confident in her skills as she seemed to shrink behind the desk's weight. A smaller, more delicate desk, made from glass or maple, would have given her the psychological appearance of being larger. Similarly, furniture in a room can make a space appear larger or smaller. Large rooms need bulkier furnishing while smaller rooms can expand in size when slim-lined furniture is used.

Kim and Tyler used the principles of scale to convert the dining nook off their kitchen into a seating area where they can lounge in soft chairs while reading their morning paper. Their first attempt at transforming the nook hit a roadblock when the overstuffed chairs they ordered barely fit into the space. The chairs encroached into the kitchen area, making it difficult to walk past them. Fortunately, they discovered a Danish company that made comfortable chairs with smaller dimensions. They added a small bistro table instead of a typical dining table to the nook as well. Using scaled-down furniture created a delightful place for reading and conversation. The space has also become the place where guests like to linger as Kim and Tyler prepare a meal, allowing the guests to be a part of the action in the kitchen and join in the conversation without getting in the way of the chefs.

Shape and Form

Instead of forcing the functions of every sort of building into one general form, adopting an outward shape for the sake of the eye... let us begin from the heart as the nucleus and work outward.

~ Horatio Greenough
Sculptor

Historically, the shape and form of structures contributed to the identity of people and the places where they lived. Forms of

buildings were often developed in response to functional needs and the impact of nature's forces. The Aztec temple in the

shape of a pyramid, the rectangular adobe structures of the Southwest Indians, or the dome-shaped igloo of the Eskimos each had distinctive forms. These shapes were closely linked to a specific place, people, and environmental condition. When the shape and form of a structure responds to its surrounding context, we are reminded of our unique identity and location in the world. This sense of identity is an important aspect of sacred design.

The tent shape of the Tabernacle captured both the essence of the people who built it and the geographical location where it was used. It provided shade from the heat of the sun during the day and protection from swirling sand and dust. In the evening as the air cooled, it offered a warm enclosure. Like many ancient structures, its shape and form responded to the environment and blended with the landscape. It was also a portable structure that could easily be transported, mirroring the movement of the nomadic people who followed traveling herds of animals. Similarly, current-day desert homes respond to the heat by incorporating long, deep overhangs that are linear in shape to block the sun from penetrating into the interior of the home. In contrast, the steep V-shaped roof pitches of homes in the northern hemisphere keep snow from building up on the roof.

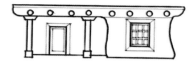

Living in a dwelling whose shape and form respond to the landscape has been Tessa's experience, a hermit who lives in a remote mountain valley in southern Colorado. Nestled near the base of the Sangre de Cristo Mountains, her circular log hogan with a coned-shaped roof sits amid slender shoots of wild grasses. Its deep wooden decks lay close to the ground as if extending a welcoming hand across the earth. The octagon shape responds well to the gusty winds that sweep across the valley in the winter, and the roof allows rain and snow to slide off its edges. The inward focus of the circular interior reflects her lifestyle of solitude and prayer and has a feminine quality to it. In contrast, Father Dave, also a hermit, lives in a dwelling not far from hers that is rectilinear in shape and seems to capture his masculine essence.

Shapes and forms emerge from the needs and activities of people as well. Chairs are intuitively placed in a circle when we gather for conversation, similar to sitting around a campfire, providing an informal sense of community. The Native American hogan, a circular

Father Dave's cube-shaped hermitage has a more masculine quality compared with the feminine circular shape of Tessa's Hogan.

structure used for community gatherings and dialogue, enclosed the people in its protective embrace. The commonly used rectangle in home design provides spaces that are easily furnished and constructed, while the oval shape of an arena works well for viewing sporting events by taking advantage of a person's natural line of sight. Shapes and forms that respond to human movement, eyesight, acoustics, and physical activities enhance a space. However, if a particular shape is too rigidly adhered to, it can begin to feel restrictive. For example, walkways that curve toward the entryway of a home and correspond to our natural movement feel more welcoming than walkways that maintain a ninety-degree angle.

I was reminded of the powerful influence shape has on the dynamics within a room when I spoke at a women's retreat several years ago. The meeting area in the facility was a rectangular room with chairs neatly arranged in rows obediently facing a tall wooden podium that stood at one end of the space, similar to the classrooms I remember from childhood. Fluorescent lights scattered across a grid of acoustical tiles overhead illuminated the room with a cool overtone. Retreat participants arrived late in the evening after a long drive along curving mountain roads and were greeted with a meeting area that felt institutional and impersonal. The space clearly didn't match the intended purpose for the weekend.

After introductions and announcements, the women dispersed for the evening. I decided to rearrange the room before the morning session, and by simply moving the podium and arranging the chairs in a semi-circle to allow participants to have eye contact with one another as well as the speaker, the atmosphere in the room immediately changed. I also used floor lamps to light the space, giving it a warm glow. Upon entering the meeting room the following morning, the women instantly responded to the changes. The shape of the furniture layout had a profound effect on the participants throughout the weekend and facilitated interactions and a sense of community among them. By adding a curved shape to the rectangular room, the space felt balanced.

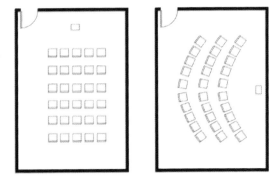

Blending shapes and forms in our homes will help it feel balanced as well. In sacred structures three forms have recurred throughout time: the cube, the pyramid, and the dome. These forms correspond to the two-dimensional shapes of the square, triangle, and circle. Pyramids and triangles appear sharp and penetrating, as if reaching toward the heavens, and have a masculine quality to them. In contrast,

domes and circles feel soft and womb-like, providing a sense of feminine enclosure. A blend of curves and angles is a blend of masculine and feminine qualities. Characteristics associated with the feminine are soft, nurturing, and inward moving while male qualities tend to be sharp, energizing, and outward moving.

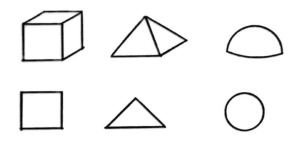

For a space to feel balanced, both masculine and feminine elements are needed. The bringing together of polar opposites in union is a creative and sacred dynamic: soft/hard, curved/angled, rough/smooth, male/female. Spaces without this balance can feel dead or cold. Just as individuals have both masculine and feminine qualities, rooms within a home need to contain both as well. Depending on the activity in a room, a particular shape or form may be preferred. An office may need crisp, clean edges, giving a sense of clear thinking and movement outward, while a family room might benefit from soft furniture and a curve-shaped ceiling, providing a soothing and relaxing environment.

The Enchantment Spa in Sedona, Arizona, combines forms in a way that complement one another. Its Crystal Grotto—a circular room with a domed ceiling—contrasts to the rectilinear spaces throughout the rest of the resort. Along the perimeter of the walls is a wooden bench that faces inward toward a water feature in the center of the room. A large crystal is nestled in the center of a petrified wooden stump, and a thin sheet of water cascades over the edges into a base of river rocks below. People enter the space barefoot and walk on a soft dirt floor the color of the surrounding red rocks. A beam of natural daylight streams through an oblong skylight from above, highlighting the fountain. Each morning guests gather for a simple ritual that includes the Native American custom known as smudging, the burning of sage. Once a week spa guests are invited to gather for a talking circle, another indigenous ritual that involves passing a stick and sharing one's thoughts. The shape and form of the space responds beautifully to the encounters that happen within its enclosure.

The shape, form, scale, and proportion of a space provide the foundation from which details such as texture, color, and light can be added. No matter how elaborate or beautifully articulated these details are applied, if the foundational components aren't in place, the overall experience in a room or space will feel slightly off.

The myriad of shapes found in nature and the classical forms of ancient architecture provide inspiration for details in our homes.

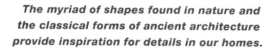

Exercises

1. Using Palladio's suggestion for proportion, take notes about how well specific rooms in your home conform to his guidelines. What materials or structural components in your home relate to the human body? For example, tiles in the bathroom relate to a hand or foot.

2. Pay attention to how different ceiling heights affect a space, particularly in commercial areas such as coffee shops, bookstores, or restaurants. Do the ceilings in your home help differentiate among the public, private, and intimate areas?

3. Notice which of the three types of shapes is prominent in your home: rectangles, triangles, or circles. Does the shape of a room work for the activity that happens there? If not, what shapes might you add to balance the room? Try including furniture, lamps, tables, or vases with curves to balance a rectilinear space.

4. Make a list of your personal body measurements using the figure below. You can also include those you live with. Knowing this information will help determine the height, width, and depth of pictures, shelves, windows, chairs, counters, and spacing at tables, that work best for you.

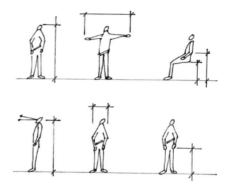

Notes

Rules of Thumb

• In sitting areas and family rooms, furniture placed in a loose circular pattern will promote interaction and visual connection. To maintain a sense of intimacy keep the distance between seating less than eight feet.

• Linear layouts with furniture against the wall work well in spaces where the floor area needs to be maximized or the room is small.

• The ceiling height of a room has the biggest impact on the overall sense of proportion. Tall, skinny rooms can be made to feel better by lowering the visual height of the room. To give the impression of a lower ceiling, suspend fabric from the ceiling or add a band of trim at door height and paint the walls above the trim the same color as the ceiling.

• Long, wide spaces can be balanced by breaking up the area into smaller segments using screens, furniture arrangements, and plants.

• The more the details in our home - such as tile, wood planks, door heights, fireplace hearths, hardware, and windows - relate to the size of your body, the better that space will feel.

Chapter 6

Architectural Details

Fill your life and your world with colors, textures, scents, and objects that are beautiful to you; that have meaning to you. Remember that we are connected to our environment. The objects and the colors in our world have energy and meaning. They have an impact on us.

~ Melody Beattie
Author

Building upon the basic foundation of architecture—scale, proportion, shape, and form—details add textural depth and vibrancy to a space. They engage us by stimulating our sense of touch and sight and by relating to our human scale. They are the bridge that helps us feel connected to our surroundings. Some details that we need to pay close attention to in our living spaces include: *Materials*, *Color*, and *Light*.

There are infinite combinations and expressions of these elements that can be incorporated into our home. How we choose to use them will depend on the mood and personality we want to convey in each room. When I was in school, I had a studio professor who harped on the significance of details in a building. He believed they fleshed-out a design, either turning it into a work of beauty or a work of mediocrity. The detail of how beam and post are connected could be a work of art or a sloppy afterthought—and it mattered. As the influential architect, Mies van der Rohe, tells us, "God is in the details." This attention to detail was evident in the work of two brothers, Bill and Steve, who were finish carpenters. Watching them work together was like witnessing a dance as they moved effortlessly, cutting and mitering oak trim, matching the grain on each board. Seamless joints gave the impression of a single strand of wood wrapping the entire baseboard and crown mold. Though it isn't something we might notice right away, subconsciously we are aware of quality craftsmanship, and it feels good. The awareness we bring to the details in our home can either enhance a sense of sacredness or diminish it.

Materials

Contrast the various materials of construction, clarify the connections among them, and celebrate the innate qualities of each rather than covering them up.

~ Jacobson, Silverstein, Murray, & Winslow Architects

Materials have an array of textures and patterns that arouse our sense of touch and sight. As infants, our first encounter and understanding of the world happened through the sense of touch and contact with the skin. If it was a positive sensation—such as a soft blanket, the warmth of a mother's body, or the smooth trickle of water from a faucet—we felt safe. Memories from this original experience of the world are reawakened through materials and textures. They are the tangible link between our body and the environment, and they have the power to help us bond physically and emotionally with our surroundings. When various textures and materials are blended in harmonious patterns throughout a room, they deepen our connection with the space.

Feng shui masters pay careful attention to the use of materials when working with the dynamic within a home. In this ancient Eastern practice, feng shui views materials as one of the primary expressions of chi—energy that animates all of life. The purpose of feng shui is to form a balance between heaven, earth, and humanity, and the materials used in a room play an important part in creating this balance in living spaces. Wood, stone, metal, and glass are representations of the five key elements used in feng shui: fire, earth, metal, water, and wood. Each element embodies a particular attribute that influences our experience in a room. By changing the materials in a space, we change the chi. For example, if a room in our home has extensive wood finishes (wood element), adding metal materials such as bronze sculptures, metal furniture, chrome light fixtures, silver candle sticks, or introducing white accents (associated with metal) will anchor the expansive quality of this element. There is an interdependent relationship among the five elements, and they are reflected in shapes, materials, textures, and colors. In general, they follow these basic guidelines:

Fire

Fire energy shoots upward and is balanced by elements of water. It is associated with the color red and triangular shapes. Light fixtures, sunlight, fire, and candles are materials that capture its essence.

Earth

Earth energy moves horizontally and is balanced by elements of wood. It is associated with the color yellow and square shapes. Ceramic bowls, stone, tile and potted plants are materials that represent earth.

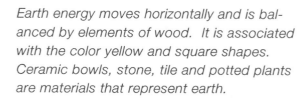

Metal

Metal energy moves inward and is balanced by elements of fire. It is associated with the color white or grey and round shapes. Metal sculptures, door hardware, hanging racks, or furniture express this energy.

Water

Water energy descends and is balanced by elements of earth. It is associated with the color black or dark blue and horizontal curving shapes. Fountains, aquariums, a clear vase, and glass block express water.

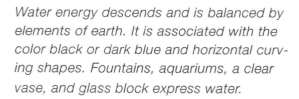

Wood

Wood energy expands and is balanced by elements of metal. It is associated with the color green and vertical rectangular shapes. Wood doors, cabinets, floor, trim, or furniture incorporate this element.

Using the principles of feng shui, we can change the dynamic in a space by introducing different objects and materials that capture the essence of one of the five elements. The relationship between the elements, as described by the following pattern, can help us achieve the harmony we desire:

• Fire enhances Earth; weakens Metal

• Earth enhances Metal; weakens Water

• Metal enhances Water; weakens Wood

• Water enhances Wood; weakens Fire

• Wood enhances Fire; weakens Earth

Here's how this might work in our home. Let's say a bedroom has a fireplace, red walls, and a vaulted V-shaped ceiling. These are all fire elements and may cause some restlessness. Adding a clear glass vase of flowers, or a painting of a stream, or a black accent pillow on a curved chair can balance the materials in the room by increasing the element of water. Earth elements such as clay vases, stone accents, and horizontal lines will also diminish the overpowering qualities of fire.

Along with balancing the types of materials used in a space, paying attention to the texture of materials is important too. Whether they are soft, hard, smooth, or rough, a variety of textures in a room add dimensional depth to the experience of a space. Just as an imbalance in the feng shui of materials can cause a sense of disconnect to a room, so can the hardness or softness of materials. This was Gary and Leslie's experience in their dwelling, which was predominantly finished in hard surfaces. Stone floors, granite counter tops, and large expanses of glass windows caused sound to reverberate throughout their home, giving it a harsh quality. Some of the rooms such as the kitchen and laundry benefitted from having hard, smooth materials for work areas. However, the rest of their home felt cold. To soften the ambience, they hung large fabric tapestries on the walls, used thickly looped area rugs in the living and dining room, included a variety of indoor plants throughout their home, and draped sheer curtains in the windows. Their voices no longer echo through their home, and they enjoy sinking into the plush cushions of their sectional couch.

Materials in our home can also connect us to the larger context where we live and to the surrounding landscape. The Tabernacle and the Native American tepee used animal skins for their structures that provided a visual and tactile reminder of their interdependence with nature. Incorporating indigenous materials into our dwelling will reinforce our connection with the natural world. This might include using local flagstone for a patio, moss rock for a fireplace, adobe bricks for exterior walls, or log beams for a ceiling. We can also use details in our home that mirror the patterns found in nature, deepening the tie even more.

Color and Light

Color and light are powerful yet simple components of space that can completely transform the character of a room. The perceived size of a room, as well as the temperature and atmosphere, are all affected by color and light. Color can increase our heart rate, calm the brain waves, or focus our attention. Combined with light, color is the most influential tool available for affecting the mood of a room. The Tabernacle used the energy of color and light to awaken the spirit and emotions within people. Golden vessels reflecting the intense desert sun outdoors yielded to a candle-lit space where an ornate curtain made from red, blue, and purple linen shimmered in the soft light. Behind the curtain was total darkness. It mirrored the natural movement of light throughout the day, from morning sunlight to the darkness of night.

Color and light are also paired in the golden Buddha surrounded by candles, the bright red entrance gate of a Shinto shrine lit up by a clear blue sky, or the shimmering aqua tiles encasing the walls of a mosque. Together they are a reminder that the holy dwells in the midst of our every day tasks in life. Even nature uses color and light to capture our attention; the bright red bloom of a cactus flower juxtaposed against an arid desert landscape or the rim of light along the edge of a cloud as the sun sets seems to invite us to pause for a moment and reconnect with our Creator. Colors have the power to stimulate our emotions and cause a variety of physiological responses in our body.

Color, light and texture can stimulate the senses and awaken our emotions. Our homes can become a haven of mood-enhancing spaces to calm the soul and refresh the mind.

~ **Anna Starmer**
Color specialist

Green, reminiscent of nature, has a soothing and balancing quality on the body and mind while strong yellows, like the sun, are warming to the body and stimulate the brain. The Egyptians and Chinese have used color as a tool for healing for centuries, and even today people seek out the healing properties of color. It can draw our attention to an object, create a sense of intimacy, or provide a serene setting for relaxation. Over time, the initial impact of color may fade as our body adjusts to a room, but color evokes a response in all people at some level. The Pink Study, done by researcher Alexander G. Schauss, documents the tranquilizing impact of the color known as Baker-Miller Pink on aggressive behavior. Offenders who were brought to the U.S. Naval Correctional Center in Seattle were put into a holding cell painted pink. Correction officers noted that no hostile or erratic behavior occurred during the initial phase of confinement for those in the pink cells.

Leslie, the mother of two small children, had a very different experience with color at her pediatrician's office. She and her son were escorted into a small examination room painted a vivid color of yellow with accents of sage green around the trim of the door. After a few minutes in the space, she became agitated by the vibrant colors and began to get a headache. When she returned to the neutral-toned waiting room, she felt her body relax. Excessive bright colors in a space tend to be unsettling. Executives have been known to paint the wall behind their desk a dramatic shade of red to minimize the length of time visitors stay in their office. Staring at a vivid red wall can be stressful on the eyes, and we subconsciously limit our exposure to the color. Having a basic understanding of color is essential for creating spaces that feel good.

In general, colors are grouped into warm, cool, and neutral tones. Warm shades of red, orange, or yellow are vibrant and energetic, drawing one's attention. The perceived size of a room will feel smaller and cozier when warm or dark colors are used on the walls and ceiling. Family rooms, kitchens, and dining areas where people gather are enhanced by warm or neutral colors. Cool colors, on the other hand, are soothing and relax our body by making a space feel larger and subdued. Using hues of blue, green, or purple in offices, bedrooms, and work areas cultivates a calm and clear environment. Neutral colors such as black, gray, white, brown, or beige, add a sense of balance to a room and work well in almost any space. The selection and combination of colors that can be used in a room is limitless and a wonderful way to give personality to a space. A few examples of the physiological impact color has on a person are listed here.

Color Guide

Red increases a person's blood pressure and rate of breathing. It also raises one's body temperature. Red stimulates the body and mind evoking strong emotions. It is the color people pay the most attention to and is the warmest color in the spectrum, stimulating appetite and energy levels. Red works well as an accent color in dining rooms.

Orange, similar to red, is an energizing color that stimulates appetite but to a lesser degree. Derivatives of the color, such as terra cotta, salmon, peach and coral, are more commonly used in living spaces. Shades of orange complement skin tones and create a sense of warmth, enhancing easy interactions.

*Yellow increases a person's metabolism and memory. Strong yellows are thought to make the brain function better but can be fatiguing to the eye and create feelings of frustration and anger with too much exposure. Babies tend to **cry** more in bright yellow rooms. Pale shades work best and can be used to brighten a room that is dark.*

Green slows the heartbeat, relaxes muscles, and decreases body temperature. The human eye is most sensitive to the color green and can see more hues of green than any other color. It is the easiest color on the eye and improves concentration. It has a balancing quality that cools a space yet has enough warmth to feel comfortable and works well in most spaces.

Blue, similar to green, is a calming color and is connected with water and serenity. It reduces a person's appetite and lowers blood pressure. People tend to be more productive in blue rooms. Blue is a good choice for bedrooms and offices but not kitchens.

Purple reduces blood pressure and suppresses a person's appetite similar to blue but feels warmer than blue tones. It is associated with royalty and luxury. Dark hues of purple feel exotic and as an accent to a room bring depth to the overall color scheme.

Though our initial response to a place is significantly affected by color, it is the quality of light that allows a room to have a variety of moods throughout the day. From ancient times, our body rhythms have been deeply linked to the natural cycles of daylight. Work, sleep, and play revolved around the rise and fall of the sun. We are so connected with sunlight that we will naturally gravitate to spaces with windows on two sides. Studies such as the one done by the California Energy Commission have shown that natural daylight increases a person's productivity, concentration, and short-term memory. To enhance our intuitive connection with light, it is essential to have several sources of light in a space. From the bright light of fluorescent tubes overhead to the warmth of sunlight streaming through a window to the dim glow of candlelight, the quality of light in a space can be subtly altered to mirror the nuances of light found in nature. Experiencing varying levels of light in a room reminds us of the natural rhythms of the earth and connects us with the internal rhythm of wakefulness and sleep.

Tracy and Carl knew the positive qualities that natural daylight adds to a space but were perplexed about how to improve a small powder room in the interior of their home. With no windows or the possibil-ity of skylights, the space felt grim and smaller than its actual size. By adding glass block to an interior wall, natural day-light was able to flow into the space from the hallway giving it an expanded feeling. In the evenings, light from the bathroom glistened through the glass block creating a translucent wall of light. Tracy and Carl were amazed at how the wall of light dra-matically transformed their dark and dingy powder room into a bright and airy space. A more modest solution would be to add vertical warm-light fluorescent tubes to either side of a mirror over a sink as a way to reflect light into the space.

Because of its versatility, light has the power to change our experience in a space very quickly. Remember the meeting room at the women's retreat? Using softer lights along with rearranging the furniture was an effective way to modify the atmo-sphere with minimal effort. The same can happen in our own home. Installing dim-mer switches to existing light fixtures is an inexpensive solution that allows us to

dim, white to colored, warm to cool, and efficient to energy consuming. Using an assortment of lighting in a space allows for a variety of moods and experiences.

Layering is a term that describes the use of several types of light in a single space. Most spaces have at least two layers of light—natural daylight and overhead lighting. Additional layers of light add depth and richness to a space as well as flexibility. In general, the more layers of light the better a room will feel. Layers include:

• Variety in the types of light sources used: natural daylight, recessed cans, chandeliers, candles, focus/spot lighting, reflected light, or wall sconces.

• Change in the heights and locations of light: ceiling mounted lights, table lamps, wall sconces, floor lighting, and cabinet lighting.

• Change in the intensity or color of the light source: dimmers, colored bulbs or shades, low voltage bulb, or candlelight.

shift the quality of light in a room to match the desired ambience. There are many options for adjusting the quality of light in a space. Using firelight, floor and table lamps, recessed ceiling lights, pendants, wall sconces, cove lighting, spot lighting, or cabinet lighting are a few options to consider. The quality of these sources of light can range from bright to

The main living space in Mary's home has several layers of light, providing a place where she can relax by herself or enjoy large social gatherings. The open floor plan and

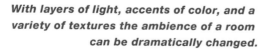

With layers of light, accents of color, and a variety of textures the ambience of a room can be dramatically changed.

variety in light sources make it easy to change the overall feel of the space. Skylights and a large arched picture window allow plenty of natural daylight to flood the space. Pendant and floor lamps illuminate tables and seating areas, and several spotlights draw attention to artwork. The recessed cans in the ceiling and the wall sconces are all on dimmer switches, which allow her to adjust the intensity of general lighting depending on the effect she is trying to achieve. If she is home alone, she enjoys using the fireplace, along with candles and a small table lamp, to create a cozy environment. Playing with the details in our home, whether it's changing the color of a room, adding velvet curtains, or adding a stone veneer to a wall affects how we feel in a space. By using a variety of materials, color, and lighting options, we can create an environment that's tailor-made for us, one that reflects our personality and our mood.

Exercises

1. List the different materials in each room of your home and note which of the five elements from feng shui it represents. Is there a balance among soft, hard, rough, smooth, and textured surfaces? Play with the feng shui concepts. Try adding objects such as a vase, rug, throw pillow, curtains, painting, sculpture, plant, water fountain, or new light fixture to change the atmosphere of a room. Or try deleting some objects if you discover that the space is cluttered with conflicting materials and textures. Do you notice a difference in how you feel in the space?

2. Take notes about how your body responds to various colors, lighting, and textures in your home. Notice which rooms feel the most comfortable to be in. Do they have natural daylight on two sides, warm or cool colors, a variety of textures, south facing windows, and layers of light?

3. Try adjusting one of the architectural elements in a room, such as painting it a new color, adding texture with curtains or a throw rug, or adding a dimmer to an overhead light. Maybe rearrange the seating into a circular pattern or place the dresser or bed at an angle. Notice the impact it has on your experience of the space. Have fun with this and experiment in small ways before jumping into major changes. Keep in mind that having layers of light, a variety of ceiling heights, colors that resonate with your needs, and proportions that relate to your body will all contribute to your sense of well-being and connection with your environment.

4. Make a Sacred Space Vision File and begin collecting photographs from magazines, your digital camera, catalogues, or the Internet of spaces that you like. Notice the colors, lighting, textures, patterns, shapes, and proportions you have intuitively selected. Include images of furniture, fabrics, materials, lighting fixtures, shapes, and patterns that capture your attention.

Notes

_____

Rules of Thumb

• Materials work together to create a harmonious balance of energy in a room. Try using the principles of Feng Shui to improve a room if it feels uncomfortable.

• Choose a pallet of three to four colors for your entire home. Use a neutral color as the primary color and accent with other colors. This will give your home a unified quality.

• Use color accents to create a dynamic atmosphere in a room. Warm colors will make a space feel smaller while cool tones will give the illusion of a larger space.

• Include at least three layers of light in bedrooms, kitchens, dining areas and living rooms. Using dimmer switches is an easy way to add a layer of light and save energy as well.

• If possible, locate sleeping areas on the east side of your home where morning sunlight can wash the room.

• Views of the outdoors provide a visual connection with nature and allow natural daylight into a space. Windows may be large or small, but a room will feel most comfortable when lit from two sides.

Chapter 7

Creating Sacred Space

Finding the sacred in everyday architecture is a discovery of the fundamental link between spirit and matter.

~ Anthony Lawlor
Architect & author

Often the most sacred moments of our life come at times when we least expect them, but we can foster an environment where they are more likely to happen. Along with using the wisdom of the Tabernacle and principles of architecture to guide us, we can learn how to use focal points, place furniture effectively, and take an inventory of our home to identify what is working well and what needs a little help to make it feel more like a sanctuary. Perhaps one of the most powerful tools we possess is our sense of play. Play opens up our mind to a myriad of possibilities and to joy.

Engage a Sense of Play

Play/making is a basic human need...it might be a project, a game, a recipe, or poem. Play is about creating or making-it involves decisions, attitudes, changes, moods, emanations, flushes, fatigues, elations, frustrations, and feelings of fullness and emptiness, tightness and lightness. When we make we immerse ourselves in time and space and material.

*~ **Daniel Mack***
Carpenter & author

When working with sacred space, rekindling a playful attitude can trigger creative channels within our brain, stimulating our imagination. It allows us to suspend practical limitations and constraints for a while. When children make forts, secret hideouts, or other special places for themselves, they see a world of possibilities hidden in the ordinary materials at hand. They engage the creative process with a sense of curiosity and are willing to be surprised by the end results of their tinkering. Vie, a seasoned spiritual director, often encourages her clients to take time for play because she believes it is through this unstructured time that wisdom emerges.

This meandering process can feel counterintuitive for adults who tend to be goal oriented, but if we engage a sense of play when working with space, the right-brain center of our body is activated. This is where intuition and creative thoughts reside. In a society that favors the logical, analytical, and verbal qualities of the left-brain function, the right brain can often be underdeveloped. But the right brain is critical when working with space because this is where visual information is processed from a spatial and expansive perspective. Solutions that arise from the right brain come from a non-verbal place. When we silence our inner critic, the right brain opens the door to an array of solutions that are unavailable to the linear-thinking left-brain. The logical part of our brain is important, but too often it stifles our powerful creative juices prematurely. We need the practicality of the left-brain to make our visions and dreams for our sacred spaces a reality but only after the creative process has begun, not before.

To help people access the more subtle intelligences within themselves, Betty Edwards wrote the book, Drawing on the Right Side of the Brain. As a drawing instructor, she believes that every individual, regardless of age or occupation, has the skills he or she needs to draw well. They simply need to learn how to release their innate abilities. She discovered that artists tend to see the world differently than non-artists. What differentiates the two groups is determined by which part of the brain they use when looking at physical forms. Betty developed a series of exercises to help her students activate the right hemisphere of their brains. By learning to see as an artist sees, students noticed marked improvements in their drawing capabilities in just a few weeks.

Schmitt, an architectural student from Bangkok, Thailand, came from a culture where children were taught from an early age to see from the right side of the brain. He could draw buildings in perfect perspective without using charts or other tools for assistance. Fellow students would solicit his help for their projects, asking him to add people, trees, cars, and other details to their illustrations. I remember struggling with one of my drawings and asking Schmitt to lend a hand. He immediately scattered my neatly packaged markers and pencils across my drafting board, telling me that being neat and orderly hindered the fluid motion of one's hands while drawing. I needed to loosen up a bit.

This whimsical bush and clay creation flow from a playful spirit.

This loosening up is exactly what a sense of play offers because it taps into the underlying creative energy that dwells within each of us. Play is an effective tool for stimulating the right brain and allows us to view three-dimensional forms and space from a broader perspective. Play is also fun. This was Siri's experience when she invited a designer to help her make some changes to her home. Though she loved her house, some of the décor was feeling tired and worn. She also had a space known affectionately as "the tree house room" that she wanted to reconfigure when her children no longer used it as a playroom. The room—surrounded by windows and located on the second floor—indeed felt like a tree house with branches of large oak trees brushing against the windows.

When the designer arrived, they wandered through her home taking in the ambiance of each room. A landscape watercolor was discovered in a stack of pictures leaning against a wall in a storage room and became the perfect focal point for a guest bedroom. An old Swedish cowbell found a new home near the back entrance. In a sun porch off the master bedroom, they sat in chairs trying out different arrangements just for fun. They held up pictures against various walls in the family room and made subtle adjustments in the placement of plants, vases, clocks, and lamps. By the end of their time together, Siri was energized and armed with new ideas for her tree house room as well as her home in general. This kind of enthusiasm is a natural outgrowth of play and is the spark that ignites our creativity.

Taking a trip to a local flea market, garage sale, or discount store can be a fun way to kick-start a playful attitude. Browsing through the aisles, tables, and shelves we might see an object that catches our eye. Jane, an interior designer at heart, has made a rule for herself to only purchase items for her home she loves. Sometimes she'll buy a piece of furniture or obscure sculpture not knowing where she'll put it,

but she trusts there will be a perfect place in her home for it. She was delighted how an old church pew discovered at an antique store and a winged birdbath converted into a planter added charm to her kitchen nook. Like Siri, we can choose

one room in our home and play with rearranging the furniture, lamps, and artwork. We may even invite a friend to help in the process, someone who has a fresh pair of eyes and ideas. The key is to keep the inner critic at bay and have a little fun.

Include Focal Points

Once we've engaged a playful attitude toward our home, we can shift our attention to the objects or focal points that anchor a room and direct movement between spaces. Highlighted objects or views help us orient ourselves in a room, giving visual clues about where to sit, stand, and move. A whimsical sculpture in a lighted art niche at the end of a hallway, a fireplace with a great aunt's painting mounted above the

mantle, or an altar displaying a labyrinth captures our attention and invites us into the space.

Janet, a spiritual director, uses an altar as the focal point for the room where she meets with her clients. An oil lamp, a cross made from sticks found at a hermitage in Italy, a singing bowl on a silk cushion, and a small tray of stones etched with words of comfort are neatly placed on a small table that sits between two wooden chairs. Each item has significance for her and helps her settle into a quiet frame of mind. They also offer a place to gaze during times of silence. Though there is a couch and other seating options in the room, the altar clearly marks where a person needs to sit during a session.

Similarly, when entering Father Dave's home, a visitor's attention is immediately drawn to his entry wall where a rich array of plaques, pottery, woven textiles, and other artwork are displayed, capturing the spirit of the Middle East culture. The objects hold stories and memories that have meaning for Father Dave and offer a glimpse into his personality. The wall reflects his work with the Desert Foundation, an organization that explores the wisdom of the world's desert peoples, their cultures, and their religions. Father Dave's passion to restore understanding and peace in the region are close to his heart. Every time he enters his home he is reminded of what he holds dear.

How we move through our home is as important as how we inhabit each space, and using focal points is a wonderful way to invite a person into a room. Traditional Japanese architecture often used a series of focal points as the primary way to direct people through a home. One might see a painting on a wall upon entering the foyer and then be drawn down a hallway toward the light of a window. A gurgling water fountain might direct a person to the garden, or a sculpture may be the focal point of a family room. Focal points make movement through our home clear and exciting.

Phil, a contractor who buys and sells homes that need remodeling, used focal points as a way to create what he called the "wow factor" for prospective buyers. He wanted a person entering the home to have at least three visual surprises, or wows, as they explored the house. In one of his projects he built a large art niche at the entryway. Moving past the art niche into the family room brought one's eye to a beautiful stacked stone fireplace highlighted with a spotlight, adding textural contrast to the sleek walls. Around the corner, the kitchen area opened up to an expansive view of the mountains through a glass wall. With every turn through the house, a person was surprised with a new visual delight. Phil knew that it feels good to be drawn into a space, and he used focal points as a way to invite potential buyers to explore the house further.

Most of us use focal points in some capacity in our home, but it is a worthwhile exercise to walk through and notice the first thing we see when entering a room; a painting might be partially blocked by the door frame, a washing machine stacked with dirty clothes might greet us when we enter through the mud room, or the view down a long corridor may be a blank wall. These kinds of details can cause a subconscious negative reaction to a space. On the other hand, we might see an array of candles on the family room coffee table, a beautiful bowl of fruit on the kitchen counter, or a birdbath in the center of a garden that acts as a reference point for pathways weaving through the vegetation. Just as focal points settle us in a room, the opposite is true as well. If a room lacks a focal point or has too much visual stimulation or clutter, it will feel tiresome and confusing.

Lighted art niches capture one's eye while the sound of water is a delightful audio focal point in a home.

The conflicting visual input will cause us to feel claustrophobic or resistant to entering a space. Clutter is like visual noise. Clearing out extraneous items in our home can turn down the volume and shift the dynamic in a room. This doesn't necessarily mean our home needs to be sparse. Bill and Jane are art collectors, and along with their artwork they display many family heirlooms throughout their home. Though an abundance of paintings hang on the walls, and sculptures, antique furniture, and antique clocks grace every room, there is an order to how they are arranged that keeps a person from becoming overwhelmed. Usually one object is the primary focal point for the room with the other pieces of art being secondary.

As the mirror to our interior reality, our physical environment can offer some helpful insights. If our home feels cluttered or in disarray, perhaps we are experiencing some interior confusion, ambiguity, or stagnation. Holding on to things that we no longer need or want or find beauti-

ful may be a way of avoiding change or moving forward in life. What we surround ourselves with does have an impact on our life, and just as focal points help us move into new surroundings, interior focus can help us move through and settle into new seasons of life. Clearing out the clutter in a room—or even cleaning out a closet or dresser drawer—can be symbolic of opening up space for something new to emerge in our life. It can help us get unstuck and invite clarity about the direction we are headed. Maybe we have a clear focus and only need a few slight adjustments, but we can play with the connection between the tangible focal points around us and our inner focal points—maybe shifting that picture a few inches will actually facilitate the shift we are hoping for within.

Mindfully Place Furniture

*Subtle movements of energy are unfolding
all the time. We feel uneasy, restless, or
impatient when we sit in one corner of a
room. We change chairs to sit in another
corner; for some reason we find it more
refreshing or more tranquil. Countless
moments like this in our everyday lives
arise from our inherent awareness of the
energies in our environment.*

**~ Master Lam Kam Chuen
Feng Shui practitioner & author**

Along with having a focal point in a room,
the careful placement of chairs, sofas,
beds, tables, dressers, and other furnishings makes a difference in how we feel in a
space. The optimum placement of furniture
in a room is closely linked to the location
of windows, doors, and circulation patterns. Feng shui practitioners often speak
of chi energy that flows through space.
The energy enters through an opening
such as an entryway and then moves
toward another opening or window as it
leaves. I like to compare it to the current
of air moving through a home when all
the doors and windows are open. Though
this is an over simplification of the movement of chi energy, it gives a general idea
of how it works. If a person is sitting in a
chair placed in the middle of the current,
she will feel uncomfortable because it will
be like having a constant breeze buffeting
her body. On the other hand, areas in a
room that are completely out of the energy
flow, such as corners, create a stagnant
area where a person just isn't drawn to be.

In the following drawings, the placement
of furniture illustrates this principle. Dia-
gram A has the chairs and table located
in the pathway of the strongest flow of chi
moving into the room. The seating area
seems to be divided in half by the stream

of energy. The chair by the window is in a particularly unsettling position. A preferable alternative, drawing B, has the furniture tucked to the side of the room where a faint flow of energy passes by.

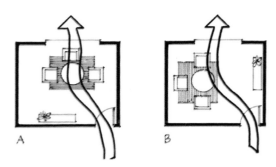

From an architectural perspective, the flow of chi often corresponds with circulation patterns in a building. Imagine a three-foot wide pathway running through a home that follows major traffic patterns, such as the path between the garage and kitchen, and hallways leading to bedrooms and offices, or simply look at the places where the carpet is worn from overuse. Furniture that cramps or blocks this natural flow will create an awkward feeling when a person moves through the room or uses the room. Another problem can arise when the circulation path cuts through the middle of a room. This was a dilemma in my current home before it was remodeled. The door to the garage opened directly into the dining room, and a person had to walk around the table and chairs to get to the kitchen. Relocating the doorway to the far end of the room and adding a bay window niche allowed the dining table to be positioned away from the primary foot traffic. Now the space feels like a separate room instead of an oversized hallway.

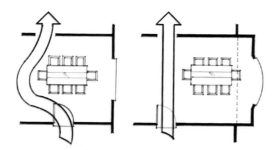

In general, seating arrangements, dining tables, or bedroom layouts that respond to circulation patterns and the flow of chi will make a room feel spacious and relaxing to inhabit. Another important component in the layout of furniture is our line of sight.

Because our visual field excludes what's behind us, we will feel more secure if a solid wall, partition, or some other barrier supports our back and we have a clear view in front of us. This is particularly important in relationship to doorways. If the doorway is behind us when we sit in a chair, at a desk, or in bed, we will feel vulnerable because our back is exposed and we can't see a person approaching us until he is inside the room. This creates a psychological sense of being on edge even if we live with people we know and trust.

Justin, who works in a wellness clinic, is keenly aware of the importance of furniture placement in relationship to the doorway. Because he wants his clients to feel at ease in his office, he has their chair situated facing the door. He says it gives them a visual exit strategy and keeps them from feeling trapped. This minor detail can make the difference between a person feeling relaxed in a room or slightly agitated.

The drawings below show how this concept works in a bedroom. The person sitting in bedroom A will feel secure with a solid wall behind his or her back and a clear view of the doorway into the room.

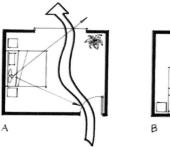

Because the doorway is to the side, it keeps the bed semi-private. There is also a nice line of sight out the window without having a direct view of the bed from the outside. In contrast, the person in bedroom B has the support of a wall behind his or her back but will feel unsettled because the entrance can't be seen. Though the view out the window may be magnificent, located directly across from the bed is not ideal. In feng shui terms, too much chi energy coming toward a person causes restlessness. It may also be a privacy issue. This holds true for doorways as well. It is best if they are off to the side without a straight view of the bed.

Sometimes it is not possible to arrange furniture ideally in a room due to the structural constraints of the space. Using window shades or adding a partition or screen to provide privacy or to redirect circulation, or even using high-backed chairs to shield one's back, are small adjustments that can shift how we feel in a room. From the perspective of our interior dwelling, paying attention to what supports us and noticing the flow of energy in our life can be insightful. Perhaps we are experiencing a nice gentle rhythm, or maybe we feel overwhelmed by too much activity (too much chi) or we lack motivation (not enough chi). Changing our point of reference or rearranging our spiritual furniture, so to speak, may give us just what we need. Alice, a graphic designer, observed that she was feeling stuck in her business, like being in a dead corner of a room. To activate her

enthusiasm for work, she decided to move her desk near a window as a symbolic gesture of inviting inspiration and a change of attitude. The subtle change in her workspace helped her get back in the flow of creativity and shifted the sluggishness she had been experiencing.

The table and tall lamps at the back of the couch creates a sense of enclosure for this seating area.

Do an Inventory

Before making any changes to our living environment, it's a good idea to do an inventory of our home in its current state. This is an information-gathering exercise that allows us the opportunity to clarify what is working well and what we'd like to improve in our home. Knowing our starting point allows us to form a clear strategy for reaching our desired goal. I remember getting a frantic call from my daughter when she was a teenager and a new driver. It was one of the first times she had driven into Denver, and she missed the exit to the Coliseum where she was competing in a horse show. The problem was that she couldn't tell me where she was, which made it impossible to get her to where she needed to be. Eventually she found an intersection with street signs, and we were able to negotiate a route that took her to the horse arena. The same is true for our home. Before we can transform it into our ideal living space, we need to know where we are. Our tendency may be to be critical of our dwelling, but the best inventory is done without judgment and is simply a fact-finding mission. We may be surprised by what we find.

A good place to start is from a broad perspective to get an overall sense of what's working well in our home and what needs improvement. Using the Tabernacle as a guide, we can assess the quality of the public, private, and intimate areas of our home. If you've been doing the exercises throughout this book, you've already started this process. I suggest beginning from the exterior of your home and moving inward. As you approach your house from outside, notice your first response. It may be positive, negative, or a little of both. Pay particular attention to the entry you use on a regular basis. Once inside, do a quick walk-through and again, be aware of what pops out for you, what you're drawn to, and what bothers you. Narrow your inventory to individual rooms and eventually to furnishings and accessories. You may even want to get as detailed as looking inside cabinets, closets, and drawers. Keep in mind the assessment tools presented in previous chapters of this book, such as scale, proportion, color, light, sound, shapes, focal points, meaningful objects, and furniture layout. The worksheets at the end of the book will help get you started. Again, this is meant to arm you with the knowledge you need to make changes to your living environment that foster a sense of sanctuary.

Another part of doing an inventory is clarifying what we want or need. Remember Bill and Emily who struggled to find a home because they hadn't articulated what each person wanted? Knowing what we want is important. It may be a general intention for the entire house or a specific idea for a particular room, such as needing more storage space, better lighting, or a quiet area. Christie, the woman from chapter one who was formerly incarcerated, has recently become a homeowner. Working with Habitat for Humanity she was able to purchase part of a duplex in a neigh-

borhood near her work. She wanted her new home to be a drug-free environment with positive energy, and with this in mind she chose to have a house dedication. A gathering of people that included her pastor, the project manager, the warden of the prison, a city councilman, volunteers, mentors, and friends crammed into her living room to participate in honoring her new space and to pray a blessing for her home.

Rose had a slightly different approach to inviting positive energy and a peaceful atmosphere into her new home. After ending a thirty-year marriage, she put her home located near the center of town on the market. She was looking forward to a new chapter in her life and as fate would have it, she happened onto a lot for sale on a cul-de-sac not too far away. It seemed divine providence had opened the door, so she decided to buy it. A few weeks later her house sold. While her new home was under construction, she had an idea to write down her dreams for her home on the plywood subfloor before the carpet and tile were laid. She invited some trusted friends, bought cans of paint, grabbed a brush and began to paint—peace, happiness, joy, a place for tears, a place where people feel welcomed, safety, and nurturing. She added some of her favorite inspirational quotes along with poems and scriptures. She doodled, and drew smiley faces and hearts until the plywood surface was a multicolored canvas of good will.

Whatever form it takes—a prayer, a blessing, or a statement—knowing what we want for our dwelling offers a focus and direction to move toward. This may also be something tangible, such as wanting vibrant colors, softer textures, more light, less clutter, or a focal point. By knowing our starting point and our desired destination, we can start taking specific actions to get us there.

Because our homes are so closely linked to who we are as individuals, doing a physical inventory of our home often reveals fascinating information about ourselves. I remember being forced to do an inventory of my storage area when the sewer backed up in my basement. Pulling out boxes of stored baby clothes, floor tiles, carpet remnants, Christmas ornaments, and other odds and ends, I discovered a large container tucked under the stair. Inside was a beautiful sculpture I had inherited from my brother who was an artist. Not wanting it to get ruined during the clean up, I placed it on the piano to keep it safe. It was stunning. I'd completely forgotten about it and was so pleased to rediscover it. Coincidently, I was in the middle of doing a personal inventory in a twelve-step program, and the parallel process was not lost on me. Just as I was clearing out my basement of damaged items or ones I no longer needed, I was doing the same with my personal life, letting go of behaviors that no longer served me. And in both processes I found something valuable that I had long forgotten.

What we surround ourselves with does make a difference. Our living spaces and the objects that fill them have an energy that affects us. A Native American healer recalls meeting with a patient who had suffered from anxiety and depression for years. Along with therapy, the healer suggested that her patient clean out his dresser drawers. He reluctantly took her advice and was surprised when he started feeling better. She knew the powerful connection between a person's physical surroundings and their internal health, and she used it in her practice to help her clients. We can also be aware of this principle when doing our home inventory, noticing the connections we discover between our physical dwelling and our spiritual dwelling within.

Final Thoughts

As we begin creating sacred space in our life and in our dwelling, we can trust our intuition to guide us and we can draw on the wisdom of the Tabernacle to direct our next steps. We can also use the principles we have learned from architecture and feng shui to bring new awareness to the details in our home, knowing that subtleties of color, light, texture, and furniture placement connect us with a room, both physically and emotionally. We can add meaningful objects to our living spaces and be mindful of our daily rituals. Writing down our hopes, dreams, intentions, or prayers for our home, or for a specific room, is a good place to start and we can ask for inspiration in the process. We can imagine the words or verses we might stuff into the walls or paint on the floors if our home was under construction. We can also listen to our dreams that have been with us since childhood.

A long-time friend and neighbor wrote the following house blessing for a family in Juarez, Mexico. Working alongside other volunteers, she helped build a simple two-room shelter for the impoverished family. After four hot and dusty days in the heart of the city, the dwelling was completed. As the family and volunteers gathered around the house, the blessing was read offering words of encouragement for the home and those who would live there. Though smaller than a garage, this modest dwelling was a safe haven in the midst of the poverty-stricken city and felt like a gift from heaven. My hope is that each of us experiences this same sense of sanctuary in our own homes.

House Blessing

As you are a God of comfort, may this be a place of encouragement and comfort, a place of being restored and replenished after long days of work.

As you are a God of peace, may this be a place of peace, of rest, of nourishment for the body and soul.

As you are a God that calls us into relationship, may this be a place of communicating and relationship, with all who live and visit here.

As you are a God of love, may this be a home of love, where there is much mercy and forgiveness, much laughter and joy.

Holy One, bless this home and may it be a place that you are welcome. Abide here in the hearts of those who are making this place their home. Thank you for your presence here.

~Kathy Narum

Exercises

1. Make a collage of objects and spaces you like but probably wouldn't include in your home because of practical considerations. This is a time to dream and imagine wild-and-crazy spaces: secret nooks, train rooms with intricate village scenes, overgrown gardens, tree houses, tepees, roof observatories, or any other kind of place that is just fun. Notice how you feel while making your collage. Hang it someplace where you can see it each day for inspiration.

2. Choose one room in your home and play with rearranging the furniture, adding some color, changing the lighting or clearing out some clutter. Brainstorm ideas about what objects, sounds, or textures would be fun to have in your space. Be sure your inner critic doesn't make any judgments about your ideas, no matter how far-fetched they may be. Try implementing one idea.

3. Describe, sketch, or create a collage of the type of altar or focal point you would place in your Holy of Holies. What objects would it include? Where would it be located in your space? Which of your five senses would it engage?

4. Check your interior dwelling. Where are your focal points? Are you feeling stuck, overwhelmed, or directionless? Make a list of areas in your life that would benefit from having more focus. Make another list of places where you have clear focus. Try adding a focal point to a room as a symbolic gesture of adding focus within.

5. Using the principles of feng shui, do an inventory of the furniture layout in each space in your home. Consider rearranging a couch, chair, dresser, or bed to better accommodate the flow of chi or the circulation patterns in your home. Notice if this makes a difference in how you feel.

6. As you go about your daily activities, pay attention to the spaces that you are drawn to and the ones you dislike, keeping in mind the tools you've learned. By tracking what you like and dislike, you will begin to notice certain patterns and qualities you repeatedly choose or shy away from. Maybe it's the color red, clean simple lines, gardens, urban settings, rural settings, a lot of light, low ceilings, soft furniture, indoor plants, or water features. Whatever you discover, it will be important to include the things that make you feel good in your home. Knowing what you don't like is just as important—these are the things you'll want to avoid having in your living space.

Notes

Rules of Thumb

• Every room needs a focal point. Try displaying meaningful objects that express your personality or adding an audio focus such as a water fountain or music.

• Altars make good focal points for personal spaces of retreat, prayer, and meditation.

• Doorways impact the optimum location of furniture in a room. In general, place seating areas with a view of the doorway.

• Avoid locating a bed on the same wall as the entrance to the bedroom. If this isn't possible, use a screen, tall plant, or add a wall two to three feet long to create a mini-hallway as a buffer between the door and bed.

• Standard circulation corridors are three feet wide. Try expanding this dimension by six to twelve inches to give the passageway a more spacious feeling without sacrificing a lot of floor area.

• When taking an inventory of your home, keep in mind the connection between your physical environment and your spiritual well-being. Make a few small changes to your living space and notice how it feels.

Exterior Worksheet

How we welcome ourselves home
and others into our presence

Entry, Front Door, Porch, Garage, Yard, Walkway, Garden				
Element	Works Well	Doesn't Work Well	Easy Fix	Major Fix
Sense of welcome				
Easy to identify				
Transition from street to entry				
Human Scale (too grand, too low)				
Variety of color, texture, surfaces, hard, soft				
Lighting				
Sound (rush of traffic, fountain, wildlife)				
Focal Point				
Vegetation (connection with nature)				
Summary of findings and ideas sparked:				

Interior Worksheet

Where we connect with others and
ourselves within our home

Living, Dining, Family, Deck, Patio, Yard, Bedrooms, Study, Nooks, Bath				
Element	**Works Well**	**Doesn't Work Well**	**Easy Fix**	**Major Fix**
Inviting (comfortable place to be with others/self)				
Human scale (right size for activity)				
Shape & volume of space (works for activity)				
Variety of color, texture, hard/soft surfaces				
Lighting				
Acoustics (does it feel private?)				
Views out side				
Focal points				
Meaningful objects				
Comfort (temperature, ventilation)				
Furniture layout				
Summary of findings and ideas sparked:				

References:

Dedication Page

Susanka, Sarah. The not so Big House: A Blueprint for the Way We Really Live. Newtown, CT: Taunton Press, Inc., 1998.

Chapter One

Kritsberg, Wayne. The Adult Children of Alcoholics Syndrome. New York, NY: Bantam Books, 1988.

Keating, Thomas. Active Meditations for Contemplative Prayer. New York, NY: The Continuum Publishing Company, 1997.

Lawlor, Anthony. The Temple in the House. New York, NY: G.P. Putnam's Sons, 1994.

Berman, Morris. Coming to Our Senses. San Francisco, CA: HarperCollins Publishers Ltd., 1990.

Chapter Two

Jung, Carl. Collected Works of Carl Jung, Volume 8. Princeton, NJ: Princeton University Press, 1961.

Chapter Three

Ban Breathnach, Sarah. Simple Abundance: A Daybook of Comfort and Joy. New York, NY: Warner Books, 1995.

Anderson, Joan. A Year by the Sea: Thoughts of an Unfinished Woman. New York, NY: Doubleday, a division of Random House, Inc., 1999.

Alexander, Christopher. A Pattern Language. New York, NY: Oxford University Press, 1977.

Merton, Thomas. New Seeds of Contemplation. New York, NY: New Directions Publishing Corporation, 1962.

Schenk De Regniers, Beatrice. A Little House of Your Own. New York, NY: Harcourt, Brace & World, Inc., 1954.

Chapter Four

Campbell, Joseph, Bill Moyers, and Betty Sue Flowers. The Power of Myth with Bill Moyers. New York, NY: Doubleday, a division of Random House, Inc. 1988.

Alexander, Christopher. A Pattern Language. New York, NY: Oxford University Press, 1977.

Ladinsky, Daniel. Love Poems from God. New York, NY: Penguin Group Publishers, 2002.

Haruf, Kent. Writers on Writing. New York, NY: Times Books, 2001.

Fulghrum, Robert. From Beginning to End, the Rituals of Our Lives. New York, NY: Villard Publishers, 1995.

Rattenburg, John. A Living Architecture: Frank Lloyd Wright and Talisesin Architects. Petaluma, CA: Pomegranate Communications, Inc., 2000.

Chapter Five

Mumford, Lewis. Roots of Contemporary Architecture. New York, NY: Dover Publications, Inc., 1972.

Eco, Umberto and Hugh Bredin (translator). Art and Beauty in the Middle Ages. New Haven, CT: Yale University Press, 2002.

Mumford, Lewis. Roots of Contemporary Architecture. New York, NY: Dover Publications, Inc., 1972.

Chapter Six

Beattie, Melody. Journey to the Heart. San Francisco, CA: HarperCollins publishers, 1996.

Jacobson, Max, Murray Silverstein, and Barbara Winslow. Patterns of Home. Newtown, CT: The Taunton Press, 2002.

Starmer, Anna. The Color Scheme Bible. Buffalo, NY: Firefly Books, Inc., 2005.

Chapter Seven

Lawlor, Anthony. The Temple in the House. New York, NY: G.P. Putnam's Sons, 1994.

Mack, Daniel. Log Cabin Living. Layton, UT: Gibbs Smith, Publishing, 1999.

Edwards, Betty. Drawing on the Right Side of the Brain. Los Angeles, CA: J. P. Tarcher, Inc., 1979.

Chuen, Master Lam Kam. Feng Shui Handbook: How to Create a Healthier Living and Working Environment. New York, NY: Henry Holt and Company, Inc., 1996.

Photograph Contributors

Randall Levensaler Photography
www.levensaler.com

Carl Yarbrough Photography
www.carlphoto.com

Anne and Bill Knorr

Jeana Krause

Dana Robinson

10677200R00095